The Problematic Self

The
Problematic
Self

Approaches to Identity in Stendhal,
D. H. Lawrence, and Malraux

Elizabeth Brody Tenenbaum

Harvard University Press
Cambridge, Massachusetts
London, England
1977

Publication of this volume has been aided by a grant from the
Andrew W. Mellon Foundation

Library of Congress Cataloging in Publication Data

Tenenbaum, Elizabeth Brody, 1944-
The problematic self.

Includes bibliographical references and index.
1. Beyle, Marie Henri, 1783-1842—Criticism and
interpretation.   2. Lawrence, David Herbert, 1885-1930—
Criticism and Interpretation.   3. Malraux, André, 1901-
1976—Criticism and Interpretation.   4. Self in literature.   I.   Title.
PQ2442.T4   809'.933'53   77-2693
ISBN 0-674-70769-9

To Gladys and Joel

Preface

Our current interest in the nature of the self reflects a close affinity with the Romantic movement, a movement that incorporated two opposing conceptions of selfhood based on contrary attitudes toward the conscious will. As heirs to a divided legacy, we still tend to maintain a tenuous balance between a Romantic celebration of a natural, impulsive self and an equally Romantic commitment to the volitional creation of a freely chosen identity. An attempt to deal fully with the role of these contrary views of the self in the nineteenth- and twentieth-century novel would probably involve a discussion of most major works of modern fiction. Instead of attempting such a task, I have chosen to focus attention on three writers who illustrate in very different ways the impact of Romanticism on characterization in the novel. While Stendhal's works reflect a simultaneous commitment to conflicting views of selfhood, Lawrence and Malraux each espouse with a rare degree of consistency one of two opposing Romantic perspectives.

The introductory chapter of this book sketches the development of two Romantic traditions. It traces the idea of the intrinsic self from Rousseau through Stendhal and Nietzsche to Lawrence, the idea of the deliberately created self from Byron through Stendhal and Nietzsche to Malraux. The scope of this study does not permit me to trace Romantic thought to its literary roots. Were I attempting a historical study, I would begin at a much earlier point, tracing the "Rousseau-istic" self to the Third Earl of Shaftesbury and eighteenth-century sentimental fiction, the "Byronic" self to Renaissance drama and Milton's *Paradise Lost.* Were I, on the other hand, concerned with Rousseau and Byron in their own right, I would devote more attention to contradictions within their personalities and their works. My use of these figures as prototypes of two sides of Romantic thought requires me to emphasize the extreme tendencies in their writing that largely determined their impact upon their contemporaries and heirs. In order to establish a fundamental pattern linking two sides of the Romantic movement with their counterparts in modern fiction, I am deliberately schematic in my opening chapter. Subsequent sections of the book attempt to do full justice to the complexity of three novelists who combine a theoretical commitment to Romantic values with exceptional insight into psychological reality.

I am very grateful to the many teachers, colleagues, and friends who have seen me through various stages of this project. Albert J. Guerard, who directed the dissertation that provided the starting point for this book, has given me indispensable guidance and encouragement over the past eight years. Herbert Lindenberger, too, has provided invaluable advice and support since the earliest stage of this study. Brenda Spatt read the entire manuscript with painstaking care. Her incisive queries and objections have led me to rethink a number of points and to clarify many others. Leslie Brisman, Stuart Davis, Emita and Speed Hill, Gerhard

Preface

Joseph, Helene Moglen, Victor Reed, and Ian Watt read sections of the manuscript and gave me a number of helpful suggestions. I am grateful to the Research Foundation of the City University of New York for a faculty research grant that provided a summer stipend and much-needed clerical aid. Finally I want to thank my husband, Joel, for helping in innumerable ways and particularly for doing far more than his share of parenting so that I could complete this book.

I should like to thank the Viking Press, William Heinemann Ltd., Laurence Pollinger Ltd., and the Estate of the late Mrs. Frieda Lawrence for permission to quote from *The Complete Poems of D. H. Lawrence,* edited by Vivian de Sola Pinto and F. Warren Roberts (copyright 1964, 1971 by Angelo Ravagli and C. M. Weekley, Executors of the Estate of Frieda Lawrence Ravagli); from *Women in Love,* by D. H. Lawrence (copyright 1920, 1922 by D. H. Lawrence, renewed 1948, 1950 by Frieda Lawrence); from *Phoenix: The Posthumous Papers of D. H. Lawrence,* edited by Edward D. McDonald (copyright 1936 by Frieda Lawrence, copyright 1964 by the Estate of Frieda Lawrence Ravagli); and from *Selected Literary Criticism of D. H. Lawrence,* edited by Anthony Beal (copyright 1932, 1936, 1955, renewed 1951 by Frieda Lawrence, copyright 1923 by Thomas Seltzer, Inc., renewed 1960 by Angelo Ravagli and Montague C. Weekley, 1964 by the Estate of Frieda Lawrence Ravagli). I also wish to thank Random House for permission to quote from *The Royal Way,* by André Malraux, translated by Stuart Gilbert (copyright 1935 by Harrison Smith and Robert Haas, Inc.), and from *Man's Fate,* by André Malraux, translated by Haakon M. Chevalier (copyright 1934 by Harrison Smith and Robert Haas, Inc., renewed 1961 by Random House, Inc.). Thanks are due the

Liveright Publishing Corporation for permission to quote from *Red and Black,* by Stendhal, translated by Robert M. Adams (copyright 1969 by W. W. Norton and Company, Inc.),and to the Van Nostrand Reinhold Company for permission to quote from *Toward a Psychology of Being,* by Abraham H. Maslow (copyright 1962, 1968 by D. Van Nostrand Company, Inc.).

Contents

The Problematic Self

Introduction

Prototypes and Continuities

The body of literature that we designate as Romantic includes two very different traditions, one defining the self as a given, the other regarding it as a creation of the will. Over the past two centuries these opposing strands of Romanticism have inscribed an hourglass pattern, converging in the writings of various nineteenth-century figures and then dividing again into contrary conceptions of identity. The two most influential figures of the Romantic movement, Rousseau and Byron, embodied diametrically opposite poles of Romantic thought. While Rousseau encouraged man to realize his nature by giving free reign to impulse, Byron inspired him to value himself for the power of his will. As heirs to both these opposing figures, Stendhal and Nietzsche maintained a simultaneous commitment to mutually contradictory views of selfhood. Nietzsche, who exerted a tremendous influence on twentieth-century thought, is a particularly important nexus in a tradition that links Rousseau and Byron with their twentieth-century counterparts, Lawrence and Malraux.[1]

Achieving an international popularity unsurpassed in literary history, Rousseau and Byron have had an incalculable impact on Western man's conception of himself. While the differences between them help to define the perimeters of

1

Romantic thought, certain core components of the Romantic approach to selfhood are reflected in their points of overlap. As unlike each other in temperament as two human beings can be, they share a self-consciousness so intense that Stendhal, a man hardly devoid of this trait himself, proposed it as a primary ground of comparison between them.[2] Rousseau's preoccupation with his own identity leads to an unprecedented achievement in self-portrayal. And although Byron seldom claims to be writing about himself,[3] it has generally been assumed that the self-absorbed figure who recurs in so many of his works is intended as a portrait of the author.[4] Nor does Byron appear to have been entirely displeased by the assumption that his immensely popular heroes closely resembled their creator. The fundamentally unchanging heroic image projected in most of his works thus suggests a repeated attempt on Byron's part to define an essentially consistent, knowable self, much as Rousseau's efforts to impose a coherent form upon the self-contradictory desires, evanescent emotions, and puzzling, irrational actions that constituted his life in fact amounts to the volitional creation of a fixed identity ratified by the public eye.[5]

Not surprisingly, however, the same faculty for introspection that enables Rousseau and Byron to project such compelling images of themselves leads them both at times not only to doubt the validity of the particular identity that their writings claim for them, but to question their very possession of a single, definable self. On one occasion Rousseau writes:

> Nothing is as unlike me as myself. It would therefore be useless to try to define myself except by this singular variety . . . Sometimes I am a hard, ferocious misanthropist; at other times, I am in ecstasy over the charms of society and the delights of love. Sometimes I am austere and devout, and for the good of my soul

I make every effort to maintain these holy dispositions: but I soon become a downright libertine . . . In a word, a Proteus, a chameleon, a woman are less changeable beings than I. This should deprive the curious of all hope of recognizing me some day by my character: because they will always find me in a particular state which will only be mine for that specific moment; and they cannot even hope to recognize me by these changes, because since they have no fixed period, they will sometimes last only an instant, other times an entire month. This very irregularity is the basis of my constitution.[6]

Similarly, Byron claimed to "have no character at all . . . being every thing by turns and nothing long."[7] If he is sincere with himself, he notes in his journal, every page that he writes should "confute, refute, and utterly abjure its predecessor."[8] After describing himself in terms of a series of paradoxes, the narrator of *Don Juan* calls into doubt the very notion of a single self: "I almost think that the same skin/ For one without—has two or three within" (XVII.11).[9]

In both Rousseau and Byron an intense preoccupation with personal identity coexists not only with an acute awareness of the mutability of the self, but also with a prototypically Romantic ambivalence toward individuated selfhood.[10] Rousseau's political theories, like his personal writings, reflect a longing to escape from discrete individuality by merging with a larger whole. In *The Social Contract* he attributes to a hypothetical "act of association" the miraculous power to replace "the individual personality of each contracting party" by a collective body possessing a common identity and a common will.[11] Unable to find the communion he so longs for within the social world, he establishes a pattern followed by many subsequent Romantics, ultimately rejecting human society in favor of a solitary communion with nature. Byron, too, finds compensation in nature for his isolation from other men. But his longing for an oceanic merging with the physical world may owe a great deal to a literary tradition established by Rousseau: tellingly, his most famous assertion of communion with nature ("I live not in myself, but I become / Portion of that around me")[12] is inspired by a scene made famous by Rousseau and followed by a eulogy to the first great French Romantic.[13]

Although certain highly visible resemblances between Rousseau and Byron—their emotional response to nature, their flamboyant personal style, their common attempt to wring "overwhelming eloquence" from personal suffering— led a number of Byron's contemporaries to link his name with Rousseau's,[14] the similarities between these two figures are less fundamental than their differences. Celebrating naturalness and spontaneity as his fundamental values, Rousseau implicitly equates true selfhood with an intrinsic nature most fully realized in the absence of volitional restraint. If, as Rousseau suggests, "our first impulses are always good,"[15] there should be little need to control our instincts by means of our conscious will. Finding support for his doctrine in his personal experiences, Rousseau writes, "All the harm that I have done has been through reflection; and the little good I may have done has been on impulse. That is why I confidently abandon myself to my inclinations."[16]

Closely related to Rousseau's exaltation of impulse over volition is his reluctance to take an active role in shaping the course of his life. "Looking ahead always ruins my enjoyment," he writes in *Confessions:* "It is never any good foreseeing the future. I have never known how to avoid it."[17] At turning points in his life Rousseau tends to abdicate all responsibility for his fate. When his friends advise him to go to Turin, for example, he eagerly places himself entirely in their hands. "By sending me to Turin they had, as I saw it,

4

assumed responsibility for my existence there," he writes. "I need have no further care for myself; others had undertaken to look after me."[18] He subsequently responds to a period of unemployment with similar passivity, giving himself "over to my own laziness and into the care of Providence."[19] In his liaison with Mme de Warens, apparently the most significant relationship of his adult life, he happily accepts a role of utter dependence: "I became entirely her concern, entirely her child," he declares with evident satisfaction.[20]

While insisting that any attempt to make him act against his inclinations turns him into a rebel, Rousseau makes it clear that his idea of liberty does not involve active self-determination: "I have never believed that a man's freedom consisted in doing what he wished, but rather [believed it consisted] in not doing what he did not wish."[21] The dichotomy between impulsive and volitional behavior so central to Rousseau's thought ultimately leads him to equate authentic selfhood with total passivity, and he finds that solitary hours of reverie, "when I leave my head entirely free and let my ideas follow their bent without resistance," are the only times of the day "where I can truly say I am that which nature has designed."[22]

In sharp contrast to Rousseau, Byron is determined above all else to shape his life in accordance with his desires. A letter to his mother written in adolescence, in which he pledges to "cut myself a path through the world or perish in the attempt,"[23] suggests a commitment to self-determination that remains as central to Byron's values as acquiescence to spontaneous impulse is to Rousseau's. Far from sharing Rousseau's love of passivity, Byron ranks the active far above the contemplative life. "I prefer the talents of action," he declares, "of war, or the senate, or even of science,—to all the speculations of those mere dreamers of another existence (I don't mean religiously but fancifully) and spectators of this apathy.''[24] While Rousseau idealizes a woman's possessive love that relieves him of responsibility for his life, Byron finds any relationship a burden when it limits his freedom of action: "It is awful work, this love," he writes in reference to his liaison with the Countess Guiccioli, "and prevents all a man's projects of good or glory.''[25]

Although both Rousseau and Byron find their greatest sense of personal fulfillment during moments of complete absorption in immediate sensation, Rousseau associates this experience with a passive receptiveness to external stimuli,[26] Byron with an active involvement in all-engrossing endeavors. "The great object of life," Byron observes, "is sensation—to feel that we exist, even though in pain. It is this 'craving void' which drives us to gaming—to battle—to travel—to intemperate, but keenly felt pursuits of any description, whose principal attraction is the agitation inseparable from their accomplishment.''[27] Rousseau likes nothing better than a serene rural existence whereas Byron can hardly imagine a less desireable state than uninterrupted tranquility; the thought of Adam and Eve's peaceful prelapsarian days leads the narrator of *Don Juan* to wonder "how they got through the twelve hours" (I.18). Easily bored, Byron finds himself unable to conceive of "any existence which duration would not render tiresome.''[28]

Rousseau's belief that the self is a given rather than a creation of the will is made clear in the opening paragraph of his *Confessions*. At the same time that he asserts the uniqueness of the man he will depict, he repudiates all responsibility for being that individual: "I am made unlike any one I have ever met; I will even venture to say that I am like no one in the whole world . . . Whether Nature did well or ill in breaking the mould in which she formed me, is a question which can only be resolved after the reading of my book.'' Significantly, we are encouraged to read the *Confessions* not to judge whether Rousseau himself has done well or ill to be the man that he is, but to decide whether the artisan Nature has done well or ill in moulding no others like him.[29]

A striking contrast to Rousseau's implicit denial of personal volition is found in Byron's celebration of the dauntless human will in his self-mythologizing play, *Manfred*. Deeply remorseful over a (presumably incestuous) love affair that led to the death of his beloved, Manfred proudly insists that his guilt has no connection with any external agent: self-corrupting, he has succumbed to no infernal tempter; self-judging, he alone defines the nature of his guilt; self-tormenting, he renders divine retribution superfluous by the anguish of his remorse. At the moment of his death he withstands a spirit's summons to hell by insisting on human autonomy:

> What I have done is done; I bear within
> A torture which could nothing gain from thine.
> The mind which is immortal makes itself
> Requital for its good or evil thoughts,
> Is its own origin of ill and end,
> And its own place and time; its innate sense,
> When stripp'd of this mortality, derives
> No colour from the fleeting things without,
> But is absorb'd in sufferance or in joy,
> Born from the knowledge of its own desert.
> *Thou* didst not tempt me, and thou couldst not tempt me;
> I have not been thy dupe nor am thy prey,
> But was my own destroyer, and will be
> My own hereafter.   (III.4.387-400)

Both Rousseau of the *Confessions* and Manfred refuse to abide external judgments of their transgressions, and both claim a fundamental innocence or guilt that has little to do with their acts. Rousseau, focusing his attention on the feelings that prompt his behavior (for example, the affection for Marion that leads him falsely to accuse her of theft in the famous ribbon incident), exonerates himself of guilt. Denying volition any role in his wrongdoing, he implicitly repudiates all moral responsibility for his actions. Manfred, on the other hand, never specifies his actual role in the death of his beloved, incriminating himself only with the cryptic assertion that he destroyed her "Not with my hand, but heart—which broke her heart; / It gazed on mine, and wither'd" (II.2.212-213). Not one to speculate on the limits of volition, he claims full responsibility for the tragic outcome of his love without seeming to attribute it to any deliberate action on his part.

It is, of course, Rousseau's conviction of his own fundamental innocence that leads him to eschew all reticence about his personal life and strive to portray himself with absolute candor. Jean Starobinski's seminal study suggests that the childhood experience of being unjustly accused and punished was the starting point of Rousseau's lifelong battle against the treachery of appearances. Abhoring whatever "veils" prevent unmediated contact with truth, Rousseau longs for complete transparence in all human relationships.[30]

Nothing can be farther from Rousseau's ideal of spontaneous self-revelation than the morose brooding of the Byronic protagonist. The aura of mysterious aloofness that surrounds this figure is viewed by his creator as an important component of his heroic stature. One of the first things we learn about Childe Harold is that "his was not that open, artless soul/ That feels relief by bidding sorrow flow" (I.8). Far from being an intrinsic part of his nature, Harold's reticence is later used as evidence of the triumph of volition over impulse:

>   to steel
> The heart against itself; and to conceal,
> With a proud caution, love, or hate, or aught,—
> Passion or feeling, purpose, grief, or zeal,—
> Which is the tyrant spirit of our thought,
> Is a stern task of soul;—no matter—it is taught.   (III.111)

In human relationships, Rousseau's longing to relinquish all defenses and engage in unrestrained communion is counterbalanced by a recurrent fear of entrapment. But he submits wholeheartedly before transcendent powers, suggesting, for example, that man should rejoice in being "merely the instrument of the Omnipotent."[31] This joyful acquiescence is later replaced by self-pitying resignation: "It was necessary to submit myself to fatality without reasoning and without revolt, because that was useless . . . since all I had to do still upon earth was to regard myself as a purely passive creature, I should not use to vain resistance against destiny the strength which remained to me to endure it."[32] But for Byron an assertive posture is always preferable to a submissive one, even when resistance is no more than a symbolic gesture. In his poem "Prometheus," Byron exhorts man to model himself after this symbol of metaphysical rebellion:

> And Man in portions can foresee
> His own funereal destiny,
> His wretchedness, and his resistance,
> And his sad unallied existence:
> To which his Spirit may oppose
> Itself—an equal to all woes,
>   And a firm will, and a deep sense,
> Which even in torture can descry
>   Its own concenter'd recompense,
> Triumphant where it dares defy,
>   And making Death a Victory.[33]

9

AN avid reader of both Byron and Rousseau, Stendhal provides a particularly interesting example of the impact of Romantic thought on nineteenth-century fiction. In his personal writings Stendhal repeatedly attests to Rousseau's influence upon him. He claims, for example, to have become "an essentially decent person" as a result of *La nouvelle Héloïse:* "After having read this book in tears and in an ecstasy of love," he declares, "I might still act like a rogue but I should feel myself to be a rogue."[34] On the other hand, he blames Rousseau for teaching him to cultivate a mode of behavior that hinders him in social intercourse.[35] Stendhal's self-conscious love of reverie would appear to constitute another legacy from Rousseau, despite the fact that Stendhal regards his daydreams with a certain ironic bemusement: "I realise in 1836 that my greatest pleasure is to day-dream, but to day-dream about what? Often about things which bore me."[36] Certain aspects of Stendhal's nature, however, are totally incompatible with Rousseauistic values, and in many respects Stendhal's temperament more closely resembles Byron's than Rousseau's. While Rousseau exalts sincerity and transparence, Stendhal loves disguise and masquerade. Ill at ease in polite society, Rousseau finds happiness in rural retreats; Stendhal is miserable whenever he is deprived of sophisticated urban pleasures. Stendhal shares Byron's restlessness, his vulnerability to boredom, his inability to find lasting satisfaction in any goal once it is achieved. While attracted to such Rousseauistic ideals as unreflective spontaneity, impulsive benevolence, and tender affection, Stendhal is also dedicated to such Byronic qualities as energy, strength of will, and daring self-assertion. Admiring Byron for much the same reasons as he did Napoleon, he once wrote a letter to the English poet praising him for breaking the "dull uniformity'' characteristic of Europe "since the death of my worshipped hero."[37]

The portrayal of Julien Sorel, protagonist of *The Red and the Black,* provides a striking reflection of Stendhal's simultaneous commitment to the two conflicting sets of values popularized by Byron and Rousseau. In certain respects Julien is a Byronic hero reduced from his quasi-mythic proportions to a size more appropriate to the novel. Dark, handsome, and proud, he scorns most other human beings even as he impresses them with his exceptional qualities. Determined to be master of his fate, he achieves the goals he sets for himself by means of an extraordinary energy and strength of will. He is also a deeply passionate man, capable of violent crime, who must bear the guilt of wounding the woman he loves. But this character has a Rousseauistic side as well. A man of generous impulses and tender feelings, he is extremely sensitive and easily moved to tears. It is, of course, the Rousseauistic side of Julien's nature that triumphs when he finds happiness in a prison cell through the love of the motherly Mme de Rênal.[38] An heir to two opposing Romantic traditions, Stendhal continually juxtaposes contradictory concepts of selfhood: he allows us to admire Julien's success in achieving an identity of his choice while suggesting that only when Julien's impulses triumph over his will is he truly himself.

THE simultaneous commitment to impulse and volition reflected in Stendhal's writing is shared by a number of nineteenth-century figures.[39] Perhaps the most explicit exposition of this paradoxical system of values can be found in the works of Nietzsche, who is probably more responsible than any other writer for the metamorphosis of Romantic thought between the nineteenth and twentieth centuries. Regarded by some as a late Romantic, by others as an early modern writer, this transitional figure provided an important link between two nineteenth-century traditions and their twentieth-century heirs. Incorporating aspects of both Rousseau and Byron, Nietzsche in turn exerted a seminal influence on both Lawrence and Malraux.[40]

In his elevation of prerational instinct over deliberate reflection, his attack on modern civilization for its departure from a hypothetical state of nature, and his belief in the existence of an "unconscious core of selfhood," Nietzsche is a direct descendant of Rousseau.[41] But, wholly unsympathetic to Rousseau's view of human nature, he feels a far greater affinity with Byron. An avid admirer of Byron's drama, he writes in *Ecce Homo,* "I must be profoundly related to Byron's Manfred: all these abysses I found in myself." So great is his admiration for Byron's iron-willed hero that he expresses the greatest scorn for anyone who would "dare to pronounce the word 'Faust' in the presence of Manfred."[42]

The Rousseauistic side of Nietzsche's thought is most clearly reflected in his esteem for natural instinct: "We must in fact seek perfect life where it has become least conscious"; "Genius resides in instinct; goodness likewise. One acts perfectly only when one acts instinctively"; "An action compelled by the instinct of life has in the joy of performing it the proof it is a *right* action."[43] Nietzsche's repeated exhortations to live by instinct alone are logically consistent with his belief that every individual has an innate (though not necessarily actualized) identity that defines the single mode of being that can authentically be his. He first proposes the notion of a unique individual destiny that is intrinsic but not determining in an early essay entitled "Schopenhauer as Educator": "There is in the world one road whereon none may go, except thou: ask not whither it lead, but go forward.''[44] This idea is restated years later in *The Gay Science: "What does your conscience say?*—'You shall become the person you are.' ''[45] Near the end of his career Nietzsche proposes himself as a model of self-actualization by subtitling his autobiographical work, *Ecce Homo,* "How One Becomes What One Is.''

If authenticity is defined by an intrinsic nature, deliberate effort of any kind may be viewed as an attempt to be something one is not, and even achievement itself becomes suspect. In the realm of creative endeavor, Nietzsche suggests, whoever aspires to distinction is inherently doomed to failure, for those who are born to greatness feel no need to strive for success. "Among artists and scholars there are many to be found today who reveal through their works a drive, a deep desire, for distinction. But precisely the need *for* distinction is fundamentally different from the needs of the distinguished soul. It is in fact the most persuasive and dangerous mark of what they lack. It is not works but 'faith' that here decides, that determines the order or rank—to reactivate an old religious formula in a new and deeper sense.''[46]

Throughout the body of his writings, Nietzsche repeatedly implies that genuine selfhood is defined by an intrinsic nature that no effort of will can modify. With equal frequency, however, he postulates a very different conception of the self, arguing for the deliberate creation of a chosen identity through the exercise of conscious volition. At one point, using a metaphor reminiscent of Shakespeare's Iago, Nietzsche describes our natural tendencies as garden plants to be cultivated by the will:

> We may be the gardeners of our inclinations, and—which the majority ignore—as richly and advantageously cultivate the germs of anger, pity, inquisitiveness, vanity, as we trail a beauti-

ful fruit along the wall. We may do so with a gardener's good or bad taste, in the French, English, Dutch, or Chinese style; we may also give full scope to Nature, only here and there applying some embellishment and adornment; finally, we may even without any knowledge and advice allow the plants to grow according to their natural growth and limits, and fight out their contest amongst themselves—nay, we may persist in taking delight in such a wilderness, though it may be difficult to do so.[47]

Far from suggesting that our nature provides a single road that alone can lead us to become what we truly are, Nietzsche here treats the intrinsic self as a source of various proclivities that we may handle as we choose in the creation of any one of a number of equally valid identities. There is certainly no suggestion now that giving free reign to one's instincts is preferable to judicious pruning. In another context Nietzsche argues even more forcefully in favor of consciously creating a self instead of acquiescing to an intrinsic nature: *"One thing is needful.*—To 'give style' to one's character—a great and rare art! It is practiced by those who survey all the strengths and weaknesses of their nature and then fit them into an artistic plan until every one of them appears as art and reason and even weaknesses delight the eye. Here a large mass of second nature has been added; there a piece of original nature has been removed—both times through long practice and daily work at it.'"[48]

By attributing all human behavior to an instinctive "will to power," Nietzsche attempts to reconcile a Rousseauistic exaltation of spontaneous impulse with a Byronic celebration of deliberate self-assertion. But instead of postulating a coherent conception of man, he in fact espouses two contradictory views of the self. The ambiguity in Nietzsche's basic doctrine is made possible by the fact that the word "will" can have two quite different meanings. In the context of the internal dynamics of an individual psyche, "will" denotes an autonomous faculty for deliberate action. But in the context of a person's relationship with external reality, this word generally refers to the capacity to struggle on one's own behalf, regardless of whether such behavior is instinctive or freely chosen. This ambiguity (equally present in English, French, and German) poses no problem for Rousseau and Byron. Implicitly equating conscious volition with aggressive self-assertion, they quite comfortably treat both as part of a single concept. Rousseau's conviction that man is by nature impulsive, noncompetitive, and desirous only of peace leads him to perceive a fundamental dichotomy between instinctive behavior on the one hand and all forms of "willful" (artificial, deliberate, or aggressive) behavior on the other. But Nietzsche, regarding the urge to dominate or control as the essence of human nature, can by no means accept this distinction. In theory, his notion of an innate will to power should overcome the dualistic mode of thought that opposes impulse and will. But instead of describing a true union between instinct and conscious volition, he alternates throughout his career between an exaltation of impulse at the expense of deliberate reflection and an exaltation of volitional self-creation at the expense of unreflecting spontaneity.

While Nietzsche consistently equates exceptional worth with an exceptionally strong will to power, his ambiguous conception of this will results in contradictory descriptions of the superior man. On the one hand he exalts those who submit without restraint to their natural leanings: "Among the noble, mental acuteness . . . is much less important than is the perfect functioning of the ruling, unconscious instincts or even a certain temerity to follow sudden impulses, court danger, or indulge spurts of violent rage, love, worship, gratitude, or vengeance.''[49] On the other hand he maintains that the strong ''enjoy their finest gaiety in . . . constraint and perfection under a law of their own.''[50] He even goes so far as to propose the ascetic as the most ''venerable'' of beings: ''The most spiritual human beings, as the *strongest,* find their happiness where others would find their destruction: in the labyrinth, in severity towards themselves and others, in attempting; their joy lies in self-constraint: with them asceticism becomes nature, need, instinct.''[51]

OVER the past two centuries the idea of a self that is intrinsic but not determining has been espoused by writers with very different notions of man's actual nature. Thus when Nietzsche urges his readers to give free reign to their instincts, he has a conception very different from Rousseau's of what kind of behavior will ensue. As Rousseau conceives of him, man in his natural state ''desires only to live and be free from labour.''[52] Nietzsche, on the other hand, imagines him striving unashamedly to extend his personal power. From Rousseau's perspective, man's only natural motive for action besides physical need is ''an innate repugnance at seeing a fellow-creature suffer.''[53] According to Nietzsche, however, it is more natural for man to cause suffering than to prevent it: life itself, he maintains, is ''assimilation, injury, violation of the foreign and the weaker, suppression, hardness, the forcing of one's own forms upon something else.''[54]

Rousseau's celebration of natural instinct, Nietzsche argues, in no way challenges traditional moral values.[55] Rousseau departs from orthodox theology primarily in his conviction that human nature is in fact intrinsically congruent with a Christian notion of virtue. Nietzsche, on the other hand, insists that the orthodox conception of postlapsarian man is more accurate than Rousseau's doctrine in its portrayal of human nature. But Nietzsche celebrates the very traits that Christianity takes as proof of man's fallen state: "In place of the 'natural man' of Rousseau, the nineteenth century has discovered a *truer image* of 'man'—it has had the *courage* to do so.—On the whole, the Christian concept 'man' has thus been reinstated. What one has *not* had the courage for is to call *this* 'man in himself' good and to see in him the guarantee of the future.''[56]

Living in an age conditioned by Nietzsche's transvaluation of values, Lawrence does not hesitate to accept Rousseau's equation of selfhood with natural instinct while ridiculing Rousseau for espousing a sentimental view of human nature.[57] Intent upon demolishing a conventional system of values, neither Nietzsche nor Lawrence takes account of his debt to the Rousseauistic tradition. But were it not for the fact that earlier exponents of this tradition had won widespread approval for man's intrinsic nature by identifying it with an accepted notion of virtue, Nietzsche and Lawrence would not have been so easily able to challenge conventional morality by declaring it incompatible with authentic selfhood.

To a post-Freudian reader any exhortation to submit without restraint to one's instinctive nature would probably suggest considerable sexual license. But neither Rousseau nor Nietzsche regards sexual desire as an essential part of the impulsive self. Rousseau does sometimes suggest that sexual morality has no foundation in nature. "I know from experience that conscience persists in following the order of nature in spite of all the laws of man," declares the Savoyard Vicar in *Emile*. "In vain is this or that forbidden; remorse makes her voice heard but feebly when what we do is permitted by well-ordered nature, and still more when we are doing her bidding.''[58] However, too much a man of his age to place sexual desire on the same plane with other kinds of impulse, Rousseau subsequently stresses the superiority of man's spiritual side, which leads to the love of truth, justice, and morality, over his physical side, which makes him a slave to his senses and his passions.[59] In writing about physical desire, Rousseau uncharacteristically identifies the self not with natural instinct but with conscious volition: "My will is independent of my senses: I consent or I resist; I yield or I win the victory, and I know very well in myself when I have done what I wanted and when I have merely given way to my passions."[60]

Nietzsche's determination to "give men back the courage to their natural drives"[61] provides an important link between Rousseau's celebration of impulse as an infallible guide to virtue and Lawrence's exaltation of the "dark gods of the blood." While Rousseau accepts the traditional dichotomy between man's physical and spiritual nature, Nietzsche insists that man's entire being is contained within his body. "Behind thy thoughts and feelings, my brother, there is a mighty lord, an unknown sage—it is called Self; it dwelleth in thy body, it is thy body," Nietzsche's Zarathustra declares. The body laughs at the pretensions of the conscious mind, Zarathustra continues, for it knows itself to be "the leading-string of the ego, and the prompter of its notions."[62] But only twenty pages after identifying the body as the true locus of the self, Zarathustra speaks with scorn of men who "know nothing better on earth than to lie with a woman."[63] In writing about sexual desire, Nietzsche, like Rousseau, tends to identify the true self not with natural instinct but with volitional control. Arguing that one need not eschew sensual pleasure as long as he is able to resist temptation at will, Nietzsche concludes, "If one's instinct is to have to succumb, i.e., to *have* to react, then one does well to avoid the opportunities ('seductions') for it.''[64] Not surprisingly, Nietzsche seems most comfortable with the idea of physical desire when he interprets it as an impulse toward domination, suggesting that male satisfaction derives largely from the subjugation of that "most dangerous plaything," the female.[65]

Since traditional religion advocates both volitional self-restraint and abnegation of the individual will, Nietzsche's "transvaluation of values" is most complete when he simultaneously demands acquiescence to one's instinctive drives and assertion of a self-determining ego. In an attempt to reconcile these opposing goals, he urges man deliberately to indulge the irrational side of his nature in order to employ it as a tool of the conscious will: ''to have and not to have one's passions, one's pro's and con's arbitrarily, to lower oneself to them, but only for hours at at a time: to 'sit down' on them, as though they were horses—often donkeys; for one must know how to utilize their stupidity as well as their fire.''[66]

Intellectual influence sometimes operates in paradoxical ways: while Rousseau's belief in man's intrinsically moral nature provided the groundwork for Nietzsche's attack on traditional moral values, it was Nietzsche's celebration of man's will to power that helped pave the way for Lawrence's exaltation of instinct at the expense of the power-hungry will. Highly sympathetic to Nietzsche's rejection of conventional notions of virtue on behalf of man's intrinsic nature, Lawrence consistently equates this nature with nonvolitional impulse. To make our passions instruments of our ego, as Nietzsche exhorts us to do, would constitute, from Lawrence's perspective, the ultimate sin against the authentic self.

On one occasion Lawrence's discussion of his own sexual doctrine includes a direct attack on Nietzsche's values. A man's contact with a woman, Lawrence declares, should give him "a sense of richness and oneness with all life, as if, by being part of life, he were infinitely rich. Which is different from the sense of power, of dominating life. The *Wille zur Macht* is a spurious feeling."[67] Even when Lawrence comes to accept the idea of an intrinsic will to power, he overlooks the side of Nietzsche's thought that parallels his own and defines his views by contrasting them to Nietzsche's: "We've got to accept the power motive, accept it in deep responsibility," declares the protagonist of *Aaron's Rod*. "It is a vast dark source of life and strength in us now, waiting either to issue into true action, or to burst into cataclysm. Power—the power-urge. The will-to-power—but not in Nietzsche's sense. Not intellectual power. Not mental power. Not conscious will-power. Not even wisdom. But dark, living, fructifying power."[68] The distinction that Lawrence attempts to make in this passage emphasizes the linguistic ambiguity that often clouds discussions of the will. To be compatible with Lawrence's fundamental values the will to power must be a purely impulsive force, unrelated to conscious volition. Combining the Nietzschean idea of an intrinsic urge to dominate with a Rousseauistic commitment to the virtue of acquiescence, Lawrence postulates the paradoxical notion of submissive self-assertion. "Anomalous as it may sound," he elsewhere declares, "if we want power, we must put aside our own will."[69]

While all exponents of the Rousseauistic tradition urge us to realize a purely instinctive self, they by no means agree on how to determine what our true impulses are. Rousseau assumes that instincts are synonymous with feelings. Challenging this assumption, Nietzsche argues that feelings derive from sources extrinsic to the self: "'Trust to your feeling.'—But feelings are nothing final, original; feelings are built up on judgments and valuations which are transmitted to us in the form of feelings (inclinations, aversions)."[70] But Nietzsche remains convinced that man can easily discover his intrinsic self by acknowledging drives that lie beneath socially sanctioned attitudes. Lawrence, on the other hand, suggests that our genuine nature may be inaccessible to the conscious mind. Perhaps the most difficult task facing Lawrentian man is distinguishing his impulsive desires from the inauthentic promptings of his ego.

WHILE the Rousseauistic tradition that passes from Nietzsche to Lawrence rests on the idea of realizing an intrinsic nature that cannot be modified by environment or volition, the Byronic tradition that passes from Nietzsche to Malraux rests on the analogous notion of asserting an autonomous will that remains independent of both social conditioning and non-volitional impulse. Although neither tradition conforms to orthodox theology, the Rousseauistic conception of the self as a given is often associated with the idea of a deity or a deified natural force. Thus for both Rousseau and Lawrence submission of the conscious will before an impulsive nature assures harmony with a power that transcends the human ego. The Byronic tradition, on the other hand, celebrates the self-sufficient individual who resolutely refuses to acquiesce before the more than human. Writing in an age when religious belief was still very much alive, Byron strongly emphasizes his protagonists' rebellion against transcendent powers. Manfred, for example, proves his strength of will largely through his refusal to submit to a variety of superhuman agents, and Cain becomes heroic through his rejection of a deity who "invented life that leads to death" (*Cain,* II.2.224).

Taking as his starting point the assumption that God is dead, Nietzsche regards man's assertion of self-sufficiency as an act of lucidity rather than rebellion. Thus while Nietzsche's Zarathustra echoes Byron's Manfred in postulating a moral autonomy that makes the individual not only his own law giver but his own judge and chastiser as well,[71] Zarathustra envisions such autonomy as a triumph not over supernatural forces but over weaknesses within man himself. The use that each makes of Prometheus, the traditional prototype of strong-willed self-assertion, reflects the fundamental difference between Byron's and Nietzsche's perspective. For Byron, Prometheus, like Manfred and Cain, represents the human spirit rebelling against transcendent powers, "triumphant where it dares defy." For Nietzsche, Prometheus symbolizes not man's capacity to resist but his ability to create, "the glorious power to *do,* which is possessed by great genius, and for which even eternal suffering is not too high a price to pay."[72]

Malraux's two earliest novels reflect a curious conjunction of the Byronic and Nietzschean viewpoints. The protagonists of these works, like the Nietzschean hero, assume that they are living in a world devoid of transcendent authority. But unlike Nietzsche, Malraux perceives man's plight in a godless universe as itself a cause for rebellion. And like Byron, he regards man's defiance of "his own funereal destiny"—the human condition—as a means of triumphing over fate. Thus Perken's pursuit of danger in *The Royal Way* as a gesture of rebellion against mortality itself has much in common with Cain's murder of Abel in Byron's play to prevent further propitiation of a death-dealing God.

The notion of volitional self-creation, which is so strikingly dramatized through the metaphysical rebellion of a Manfred, Prometheus, Cain, Garine, or Perken, becomes problematic indeed as soon as one demands a firmer foundation for identity than symbolic gestures of defiance. The common Romantic assumption that the individual must find a basis for his existence independent of social values and traditional beliefs is easier to deal with from a Rousseauistic than from a Byronic perspective. Neither Rousseau's nor Lawrence's heroes need concern themselves with finding an object for their actions, which require no further justification than the fact of having been prompted by an intrinsic desire. Similarly, when Stendhal and Nietzsche approach the self as a given, they encourage us to believe that natural instinct can provide sufficient direction for human lives. But Byron's and Malraux's protagonists (as well as those of Stendhal and Nietzsche insofar as they are self-creating rather than self-actualizing figures) are faced with the burden not only of realizing a chosen identity, but of finding values upon which their choice of an identity can rest.

The problem of defining an adequate basis for self-creation is implicit in Byron's *Manfred,* whose unyielding protagonist can ultimately find no goal except oblivion. Stendhal's heroes, like Byron's, are frequently characterized by a powerful will that can find no meaningful object. The only means of self-creation at their disposal is the pursuit of success within a society that they despise. Nietzsche generally avoids facing the question of how to find a basis for choosing an identity by simply defining the "superior" man with whom he is concerned as one who creates his own values. But a character in *Thus Spake Zarathustra* who repudiates all conventional beliefs only to wander aimlessly, devoid of any goal, is significantly named Zarathustra's shadow.[73]

Very much a disciple of Nietzsche while writing his first two novels, Malraux attributes to his early protagonists a hunger for power that leads to single-minded dedication to goals chosen almost at random. In subsequent works, however, no longer satisfied with actions whose only purpose is self-assertion, Malraux suggests that a concern for the fate of one's fellows provides the most meaningful basis for the creation of a self. Thus only by repudiating Nietzsche's disdain for the common man can Malraux find an adequate object for the volitional self-assertion that Nietzsche taught him to value so highly.[74]

WITHIN both the Rousseauistic and the Byronic tradition, there has been a progression from an implicit acceptance of certain underlying assumptions toward a greater awareness of the problematic nature of any conception of the self. Literature of the Romantic period tends automatically to identify certain kinds of behavior with impulse, others with volition. Thus while Rousseau exalts certain states of being as inherently more natural than others, Byron repeatedly endorses a particular self-presentation as proof of an iron will. The fact that the typical Byronic hero is a moody, tempestuous man plagued by self-generated anguish might seem to undercut Byron's emphasis on his deliberate self-determination. But the relationship between volitional self-assertion and psychological need is no more a problem for Byron than the source of man's benevolent feelings is for Rousseau.

An immediate successor to both Rousseau and Byron, Stendhal distinguishes between spontaneous and volitional behavior on the basis of assumptions that he shares with both. Like Rousseau he associates tenderness, compassion, a love of beauty, and a proclivity to daydream with an intrinsic nature; like Byron he identifies energy, pride, and rebelliousness as manifestations of a self-creating will. Thus, for example, he suggests that Julien Sorel acts more naturally when he responds to beautiful scenery or tender affection than when he strives for honor, recognition, and power, despite the fact that Julien's need for achievement strikes the reader as the dominant force in his psychological makeup.

Dismissing such Rousseauistic values as tender benevolence and passive reverie as an inadequate basis for human behavior, Nietzsche alternately identifies the assertive action that he values so highly with unreflecting impulse and deliberate volition. Even the self-control that makes an individual master of his impulses is sometimes portrayed as a genuine capacity for choice, sometimes as a drive no less instinctive than any other. Thus Nietzsche's concept of a will to power embraces behavior ranging from aggressive self-aggrandizement to ascetic self-restraint, regardless of whether such behavior derives from an internal compulsion or a truly volitional choice.

Both Lawrence and Malraux devote considerably more attention than their predecessors to problems involved in distinguishing impulse from volition. Lawrence is aware, for example, that an intellectual commitment to impulsive behavior leads some individuals to will themselves to act "instinctively." Thus Hermione argues in favor of passion and the instincts in *Women in Love* only to be told by Birkin that her real goal is the mental pleasure of observing her own animalism. Certain individuals, Lawrence suggests, are incapable of true self-abandon; their "deliberate spontaneity" is unrelated to their deepest nature.

While seemingly instinctive behavior can be the product of conscious effort, "willed" behavior may in fact derive from nonvolitional impulse. Both Lawrence and Malraux suggest on several occasions that characters who pride themselves on their self-possession may be forced to act as they do by compelling emotional needs. Both novelists, furthermore, associate an obsession with the power of one's will with an unacknowledged wish for death. Like *Manfred* and *The Red and the Black*, *Women in Love* and *Man's Fate* each depict the virtual suicide of an exceptionally strong-willed figure. But unlike Byron and Stendhal, Lawrence and Malraux explicitly relate this character's strength of will to a self-destructive impulse that dooms him.

1

Stendhal

Simultaneously devoted to logic and passion, dryness and tenderness, elegance and energy, Stendhal is a paradoxical figure in many respects. He emphasizes the role of environment in the formation of personality yet repeatedly creates protagonists who transcend all cultural norms; and he admires with equal intensity wholehearted acquiescence to impulse and vigorous assertion of the will. Incorporating opposite aspects of the Romantic movement, his novels reflect two conflicting attitudes toward conscious volition and two contradictory definitions of the self.

Stendhal was as eager to escape or transform his own identity as he was to understand and define it. The pen name by which he is generally known is one of well over a hundred pseudonyms employed by Henri Beyle in what appears to have been a lifelong game of masquerade.[1] Jean Starobinski attributes Stendhal's fondness for personal inconsistencies and disguises to a desire to free himself from any identity that others might impose upon him.[2] But Stendhal's proliferation of ever-changing public selves was perhaps also an attempt to compensate for the stable private self that he tried in vain to find.

Although his efforts at autobiography were deeply influenced by Rousseau's *Confessions,* Stendhal was more skeptical than Rousseau about the possibility of attaining total self-knowledge.[3] In *Memoirs of Egotism* he declares, "It is possible to understand everything except oneself."[4] Nevertheless, to understand himself as thoroughly as possible was one of his primary goals, and he claims to write *The Life of Henry Brulard* in the hope that "perhaps I shall at last know, when it's finished, in two or three years' time, what sort of man I have been, gay or gloomy, wit or fool, brave man or coward, and, all things considered, happy or unhappy."[5]

At the age of twenty-three Stendhal wrote in his diary, "I ought to examine myself thoroughly so as to find out what I ought to desire."[6] Some thirty years later, in *The Life of Henry Brulard,* he reverses the procedure suggested here. No longer assuming that knowledge of himself can tell him what to desire, he now views his desires as the only available index of his identity: "I don't know what I am: kind, unkind, witty or foolish. But I do know perfectly well what gives me pain or pleasure, what I desire and what I hate" (p. 216). Unable to perceive his own character traits, Stendhal attempts to use his personal likes and dislikes as an alternative basis for self-definition, claiming with obvious satisfaction that his fundamental values have remained constant since his childhood: "Forty-two years ago, my way of pursuing happiness was exactly the same as it is today, in other and more familiar terms my character was absolutely the same as today" (p. 83). Subsequently, however, he is reduced to a rather more limited claim: "I adored Saint-Simon in 1800 as I do in 1836. Spinach and Saint-Simon have been my only lasting tastes, next, however, to my taste for living in Paris with a hundred louis a year, writing books" (p. 323).

Stendhal's attempt to derive a sense of identity from his personal tastes cannot ultimately withstand his awareness that such tastes are frequently transient and sometimes spurious. When Stendhal left home at the age of sixteen, he was amazed to find himself indifferent to both Paris and mathematics, the two things he had formerly desired above all else. This experience led him to distrust at times even the most intense of feelings. In *Lucien Leuwen* Stendhal describes the terror of a young man who discovers that his emotions are totally unpredictable. Suddenly (and temporarily) bored by Mme de Chasteller, Lucien declares, ''Tomorrow I may become an assassin, a thief, anything at all! For I am sure of nothing about myself.''[7]

Not only is it impossible to predict the future of a passion, but even those feelings that remain constant over a long period of time may be an unreliable index of one's true tastes. After a careful analysis of his musical preferences, Stendhal declares, ''One is always a bad judge of one's own passions or tastes, particularly when these tastes are fashionable ones.''[8] By suggesting that an individual acting in good faith cannot distinguish between tastes that are dictated by fashion and those that are truly his own, Stendhal implies that among the feelings one actually experiences, some are inherent and therefore genuine while others are culturally conditioned and hence not truly a part of the self. A similar point is raised near the beginning of *The Red and the Black* with regard to Julien's determination to accept no position that necessitates his eating with servants. The narrator declares, ''This horror of eating with servants was by no means natural to Julien; in order to make his fortune he would have done other things much more painful in themselves. He had picked up this notion from Rousseau's *Confessions*.''[9] Julien's revulsion may not be innate, but his emotion is certainly genuine. A large number of Julien's values and convictions seem to derive from his early reading: deprived of all

29

literary influences, he would presumably have been a very different man. Must we subtract all Napoleonic ambitions and all Rousseauistic sensibilities in order to define Julien's true identity, or are we to conclude that certain kinds of influence become incorporated into one's nature, while others lead only to superficial attitudes with no real bearing upon the self?

Throughout his life Stendhal had great admiration for the philosopher Destutt de Tracy,[10] whose Lockean emphasis on environmental conditioning is reflected in one aspect of Stendhal's conception of personal identity. In his treatise on love Stendhal maintains that our most fundamental likes and dislikes are products of parental influence. "The imitativeness of our early years makes us acquire the passions of our parents, even when these passions poison our lives." "From the age of six we become accustomed to seek happiness along the same paths as our parents."[11] But if, as these passages suggest, Stendhal assumes that all tastes are learned rather than innate, he must distinguish between feelings that are "natural" to us and equally intense feelings that are not by setting an arbitrary time limit on the development of our nature. On one occasion Stendhal explicitly defines an individual's true character as the part of his personality created by early experience. In *The Red and the Black* he writes of M. de La Mole: "Under these strange circumstances his fundamental character, which had been established by the events of his youth, resumed its sway" (p. 356). Even behavior that appears to be purely instinctive is sometimes attributed to environmental influence. "In this moment of passion," Stendhal writes in *The Charterhouse of Parma*, "Fabrizio forgot everything he had ever learned of the laws of honour and reverted to instinct, or, more properly speaking, to the memories of his earliest childhood."[12]

Stendhal's interest in the process by which childhood experiences shape adult character is clearly reflected in *The Life of Henry Brulard.* He traces his moral values to his reading of Rousseau, his "Spanish" sensibility to the influence of a great-aunt, and his political and religious rebelliousness to specific events of his early years. His belief that our strongest likes and dislikes are patterned upon those of our parents helps him explain a fundamental contradiction within his adult values. When Stendhal was a child, the influence of his politically conservative family undermined his theoretical convictions: "In spite of the perfectly and essentially republican views I held at that time, my relatives had successfully imparted to me their aristocratic and stand-offish tastes." For the rest of his life, an unconquerable hatred of vulgarity conflicted with his democratic principles: "I loathe the mob (to have any dealings with), while at the same time I passionately desire their happiness as *the people*" (p. 116).

The theory of childhood conditioning enables Stendhal to account for certain aspects of his character of which he does not entirely approve. But it does not explain why he became in many respects so different from his relatives. Stendhal responds to this logical problem by blaming not his theory but his guardians: "If my relatives had known how to manage me, they could have turned me into the kind of simpleton I see so often in the provinces. The indignation I have always felt, ever since my childhood and with the greatest intensity, formed my character, such as it is, in spite of them" (p. 156). Under normal circumstances, Stendhal suggests, parents have almost total power in the shaping of their offspring. But parental figures as despicable as Stendhal's father and aunt constitute an exception to this rule, for they inspire in their youthful captive a rage potent enough to negate their influence upon him.

Although Stendhal is pleased to have largely resisted the values of his immediate family, he by no means regards all external influence as something to be eschewed. In fact he repeatedly complains because various men he admired in his youth failed to give him the guidance he rejected from those at home: "M. Rebuffel could have made anything he liked of me," he writes. "I would have been a wiser man if chance had set me under his direction. But it was my destiny to have to fight for everything" (pp. 303-304). Similar in tone are two passages, both beginning with the phrase "How different it would have been," in which Stendhal blames his well-meaning Uncle Daru for failing to impart to him the secrets of either social success or epistolary grace (pp. 299, 310). Michael Wood regards the surprising desire for counsel repeatedly expressed in *The Life of Henry Brulard* as a sign of Stendhal's fatigue as he approaches the final years of an exhausting life, "a first stirring of the desire for someone else to take over."[13] Whatever its cause, Stendhal's emphasis on his lack of early guidance is part of a general concern with formative influences that is more pronounced here than in his other works. Devoting little attention to either intrinsic impulse or conscious volition, Stendhal traces his own identity largely to contingencies that govern the impact of the world upon the self.

Autobiographical writing by its very nature tends to involve a search for links between past and present, for underlying causes that can explain the course of one's life.[14] But Stendhal's emphasis in *Henry Brulard* on forces external to his will goes far beyond that dictated by his task. Near the beginning of this work Stendhal writes, "After all, I said to myself, I haven't spent my life too badly . . . *spent* it? Oh, that's to say, chance has not inflicted too many misfortunes on me, for have I, in fact, had any control at all over my life?'' (p.2). The fatalism that pervades *Henry Brulard* is not surprising when we consider the circumstances under which this book was written. Obliged by financial necessity to accept a diplomatic appointment not at all to his liking, Stendhal succinctly summarizes his own predicament when he writes, ''Think of being obliged to tremble for the retention of a post at which one perishes of boredom!''[15] Stendhal's immediate situation, which mocks his lifelong devotion to the pursuit of happiness, gives him little reason to see himself as the master of his fate.

Although in *Henry Brulard* Stendhal treats personal identity largely as a product of external influences, elsewhere he emphasizes an intrinsic self that remains immune to all conditioning forces. On one occasion he compares a man's natural character to a granite rock, his acquired habits to ''vegetative fill,'' maintaining that ''politeness, the way of the world, and prudence'' cover the contours of the granite, producing a smooth surface that a young man mistakes for a plain. ''He does not see that, as soon as the man must do something he considers important, he will follow the contour of the *granite* in his character.''[16]

The relationship between what Stendhal here calls ''granite'' and ''fill'' is a recurrent theme in his writings. At the age of twenty-two he writes in his diary that his desire for worldly success is an acquired taste that will be quickly satiated, leaving the core of his being untouched: ''A year of luxury and the pleasure of vanity, and I'll have satisfied the needs given me by the influence of my century, I'll return to the pleasures which are really pleasures for my soul, and with which I'll never be disgusted'' (p. 100). But several years later he is less optimistic about the relative power of nature and nurture. Discovering that he is unable to overcome ambition and pursue only happiness, he realizes that his society has had a lasting effect upon him. "This is a sin against *Bey-lism*," he writes to a friend. "It is a result of the execrable moral education we received. We are orange-trees that have sprouted up, by the strength of their seed, in the middle of a pool of ice, in Iceland."[17] But even as Stendhal acknowledges that ignoble motives determine his actual behavior, his imagery claims him to be inherently superior to the world into which he was born.

Closely related to Stendhal's conception of an intrinsically admirable self corrupted by society is his Rousseauistic commitment to impulsive behavior.[18] His obvious approval of his fictional protagonists at moments when socially sanctioned roles are discarded and deliberate self-creation fails (for example, when Julien falls at Mme de Rênal's feet) celebrates a part of the self that is independent of both culture and volition. In *Lucien Leuwen* he argues for unpredictable spontaneity, castigating uniformity of temper as "the masterpiece of that hypocrisy which is known today as a perfect education . . . and which makes for an incurable dullness in the person who practices it" (II, 343).

When Stendhal contrasts "natural" with socially conditioned behavior, he almost always argues for the former. But unlike Rousseau he does not make transparency his ultimate ideal. His sympathetic depiction of characters like Count Mosca and the senior Leuwen, hardly models of ingenuous sincerity, reflects the admiration for conscious self-creation that continually counterbalances his esteem for natural impulse. Unlike Rousseau, who hates all forms of pretense and concealment, Stendhal distinguishes between two kinds of artifice. Bourgeois hypocrisy is always judged by Rousseauistic standards and inspires Stendhal with a passionate love of the natural. But in the presence of aesthetically perfect artifice, ingenuous transparency, though still praised, somehow appears to be a rather amorphous virtue.[19]

A triple allegiance to impulse, culture, and volition is reflected in Stendhal's treatise on love. This work repeatedly describes its subject as a purely spontaneous, involuntary state: "Love is like a fever which comes and goes quite independently of the will" (p. 32). "It is easy to see from this that the will has no control over love" (p. 58). "Nothing is so interesting as passion; everything about it is so unexpected, and its agent is also its victim. Nothing could be duller than mannered love, where everything is calculated" (p. 183). Elsewhere, however, Stendhal suggests that love is less instinctual than learned. Its pleasures, he maintains, derive largely from delicate refinements: "Love is civilization's miracle. Among savages and barbarians only physical love of the coarsest kind exists" (p. 61).[20] Stendhal recognizes that feminine modesty is not an inherent trait, but his own preference for modest women convinces him that, at least in this one respect, civilization has improved upon nature: "Clearly, modesty is largely something that is learnt. It is perhaps the only law begotten by civilization which engenders nothing but happiness" (pp. 60-61). Totally "natural" behavior in the presence of one's beloved is prevented, Stendhal argues, not only by social conditioning but also by the desire to make a good impression. The lover "is aware of the enormous weight attaching to every word he speaks to his beloved, and feels that a word may decide his fate. He can hardly avoid trying to express himself well, nor, if he succeeds, can he help feeling that he *is* speaking well. From that moment candour is lost. There must, therefore, be no pretensions to candour, which is a characteristic of those who are not turned in upon themselves. We are what we succeed in being, but we are conscious of what we are'' (p. 84).[21] The identity we create for ourselves by deliberate choice is no less genuine, Stendhal suggests, than the one given us by our instincts or our culture.

Stendhal's portrayal of fictional characters reflects many of the same tensions and contradictions that are found in his nonfictional discussions of the self. But social conditioning plays a considerably smaller role in the depiction of his protagonists than it does in his theoretical statements about personal identity. As both Erich Auerbach and George Lukács point out, the capacity of the Stendhalian hero to transcend the influence of his environment is what most clearly distinguishes Stendhal from other French ''realists.''[22] Like his Romantic predecessors, Stendhal assumes that the superior individual will largely escape the influence of a corrupt and corrupting world. But, unlike them, he entertains no dreams of withdrawing from society altogether, for he cannot imagine a satisfactory alternative to the urbane environment he so enjoys. Lucien Leuwen expresses his creator's tastes when he declares, ''I need the pleasures of a time-honored civilization.'' But a moment later he expresses Stendhal's harsh self-judgment as he adds, ''Well then, donkey, why don't you support the corrupt governments which are the products of civilization? Only a fool or a child is content to harbor two conflicting desires at the same time'' (I, 71).

THE portrayal of Julien Sorel in *The Red and the Black* owes much of its complexity to Stendhal's ambivalence regarding, on the one hand, the relationship between the individual and his society and, on the other, the conflicting forces of intrinsic impulse and conscious volition within the individual himself. Like a long line of Romantic figures, including both the Jean-Jacques of Rousseau's autobiographical writing and the typical Byronic hero, Julien Sorel is depicted as a man at odds with his society. Constitutionally unfit for the rough, brutal life to which his origin consigns him yet forever alienated by his birth from all classes above his own, Julien is doomed to be ill at ease in any social milieu. From the vantage point of a perpetual outsider, he clearly perceives the meanness, hypocrisy, and corruption that pervade every level of society. But like his creator he finds it impossible to preserve his integrity by totally repudiating the social world.

Intensely ambitious, Julien regards worldly success as the only reliable verification of a personal superiority that he feels compelled to prove.[23] His sense of his own worth thus comes to rest upon the judgment of a society whose values he despises. Early in his career Julien is forced to decide whether to accept a partnership in his friend Fouqué's lumber business or pursue his own plans for achieving public glory. He attempts to justify his rejection of Fouqué's proposition by contrasting the "comfortable mediocrity" that his friend has offered him with "the heroic dreams of youth" that he still hopes to fulfill. But in his more lucid moments Julien recognizes that these dreams have no basis in reality, for the world in which he must make his way has little interest in heroes. Observing that a young vicar has the power to corrupt a respectable old justice of the peace, Julien resolves upon an ecclesiastical career as the surest road to success.

Even though Julien has little inclination to accept Fouqué's offer, the unprecedented sense of freedom that it gives him results in temporary elation: "His chance of getting ahead in the world with Fouqué gave a certain fluency to Julien's speculations; they were not now spoiled so often by irritation and a bitter sense of poverty and contempt in the eyes of the world. Placed as it were on a lofty promontory, he could judge and exercise dominion, so to speak, over the alternatives of extreme poverty and the comparative comfort he called wealth. He was far from taking stock of his position like a philosopher, but he had enough insight to feel that he was *different* after his brief trip through the mountains'' (p. 60). But a short while later we find him in quite another mood: "Julien was sullen all evening; hitherto, he had been angry only with his destiny and with society, but since Fouqué had offered him a vulgar way to wealth, he was angry with himself as well'' (p. 62). Before Fouqué offered him a partnership, Julien had been convinced that an ecclesiastical career was his only alternative to an unbearable existence in Verrières. The hypocrisy and cunning necessitated by his ambition were, he formerly believed, forced upon him by a world that offered no honorable path to independence. Once Julien is given the opportunity of supporting himself with a respectable trade, he can no longer blame his circumstances for the course he elects to follow. His sudden and irrational dissatisfaction with himself suggests an awareness (though perhaps not a fully conscious one) that once he rejects Fouqué's proposal, whatever compromises his career requires must be accepted as part of a freely chosen identity.

Stendhal's handling of this episode is typical of his subtle and often elliptical approach to character portrayal. He explains in considerable detail the elation that one would expect Julien to feel as a result of Fouqué's offer. But when Julien's mood changes to depressed irritation, Stendhal is far less explicit in his analysis, leaving it to the reader to deduce why Fouqué's offer, at first a source of intense gratification, should suddenly make Julien so dissatisfied with himself.

Determined to make a name for himself at any cost, Julien realizes that he will have to do so on society's terms. The values that he has derived from his avid reading of Rousseau's *Confessions,* bulletins from the Grande Armée, and the *Mémorial de Sainte-Hélène* are worse than useless to an aspiring young man in the France of 1830. Ecclesiastical preferment, the one accessible means to social mobility, is hardly to be gained by emulating the revolutionary fervor of Napoleon or the self-revealing candor of Rousseau. To satisfy his ambition Julien must construct a public identity that bears no relation to his genuine feelings and beliefs: in other words, he must become a hypocrite. But in affixing this label to him it is important to draw a clear distinction between two very different meanings of the word.[24] The kind of hypocrisy exemplified by such characters as George Eliot's Bulstrode and Charles Dickens's Pecksniff is a totally different phenomenon from Julien's. Both Bulstrode and Pecksniff are public exponents of a morality that does not in fact govern their behavior. But each of them actually shares the perspective of his society and wishes to embody the morality he professes. Pecksniff seems totally unaware of the discrepancy between his principles and his actions, while Bulstrode tries to forget his failure to live up to his ideals. Julien, on the other hand, having never assimilated the values of his society, has no desire to possess the conventional virtues he claims. His position as a perpetual outsider thus enables him to deceive others without deceiving himself.[25]

Of course, Julien does not always succeed in his attempts to create a public self tailormade for the achievement of his goals. Despite his constant effort to appear humble and pious, even the innocent Abbé Chélan perceives in him a worldliness not befitting a priest. Subsequently, Julien's stratagems at the Besançon seminary prove totally inept, and Stendhal suggests that he is too naive to be truly hypocritical: "All the first actions of our hero, who considered himself such a politician, were, like his choice of a confessor, acts of folly. Misled by the presumption natural to an imaginative man, he mistook his inward intentions for outward acts and considered himself a consummate hypocrite" (p. 141). A man is to be defined by the results rather than the motives of his acts, Stendhal implies, and one is a true hypocrite only if one's ruses succeed.

Despite his occasional clumsiness, Julien is generally successful in achieving the public image that his goals require. Had he been less skillful at disguising his true feelings, he would never have gotten his job as tutor to M. de Rênal's children, much less his position in the de La Mole household. Thus only by freeing his public identity from his private self can Julien escape the fate imposed by his plebeian birth. But the hypocrisy that makes possible Julien's social rise is, from another perspective, a barrier to freedom. Ostensibly an expedient to be employed at will, self-concealment becomes a psychological necessity. Determined to keep his public self an artifact of his will, Julien finds it impossible to be at ease with anyone: "his hypocrisy prevented his feeling free even with Fouqué" (p. 57). Assuming that he can win approval only by perpetual disguise, Julien strives to fulfill what he takes to be the expectations of those around him. At one point relaxing his will sufficiently to speak to Mme de Rênal of his admiration for Napoleon, he instantly perceives her disapproval. Since he has come to regard hypocrisy as his only defense, Julien never considers the possibility of explaining his point of view. Instead he resolves never again to expose his true beliefs to his mistress. Had he attempted to explain himself, he would have found Mme de Rênal a most sympathetic listener: "Julien's happiness that day was on the verge of becoming lasting. Our hero simply lacked the audacity to be sincere" (p. 74).

Near the end of the novel Julien declares that the habit of insincerity even permeates his private thoughts: "The influence of my contemporaries is stronger than I am, he said aloud, and with a bitter laugh. Talking in solitude to myself,

only two steps away from death, I am still a hypocrite . . . O
nineteenth century!'' (p. 402). The reader is apparently intended to accept this declaration at face value, but Stendhal
relies on rhetoric to make a point that is not convincingly
dramatized. Julien's bitterness springs from the realization
that he has misunderstood his own emotions. Having attributed his melancholy mood to imminent death, to the
dungeon, to damp air, he suddenly identifies Mme de
Rênal's absence as the true cause of his despair. But to suppress a disturbing thought is a normal human impulse, and
Julien's temporary lack of insight hardly justifies his vehement denunciation of society and self. Moreover, a man who
spots self-deception so quickly and hates it so intensely seems
to have little reason to accuse his age of destroying his integrity. Stendhal's criticism of the nineteenth century might have
appeared more valid if its corrupting power had been de-
nounced by the narrator rather than by its putative victim.
But ever since the shooting of Mme de Rênal, Julien has been
treated with the respect befitting a Romantic outlaw, and the
narrator could not accuse him of self-deception without
undermining his newly attained stature. Stendhal attempts
to demonstrate that Julien, although a victim of the corrupting influence of his society, remains superior to his fate
because he can judge both himself and the world that corrupted him. But because Stendhal fails to create an adequate
dramatic context for his rhetoric, we are less likely to admire
Julien's lucidity than to wonder if he is not a bit too ready to
blame society for his own inability to live up to an unrealistic
ideal.

IT has been observed that the system of values upheld by
most nineteenth-century novels is that of a merchant class far
more interested in honesty than in honor.[26] But Stendhal,

ever disdainful of middle-class morality, creates a hero who regards deception as a legitimate tool but values honor above all else. Even Julien's ambition, which overrides all ethical scruples, loses its power when he believes his honor to be at stake. Shortly after arriving in Besançon Julien attracts the interest of a local waitress, earning a rude stare from her lover. Julien is ready to sacrifice his career to avenge this dishonor: "It was in vain that prudence reminded him: Fight a duel the day you come to Besançon and your career in the church is over" (p. 132). Dissuaded from pursuing a ridiculous quarrel, Julien later looks back remorsefully upon his failure to fight. When a coachman's theft of his master's calling cards subsequently provides Julien with an opportunity to prove that he is a man of honor, he finds dueling as disappointing as love. "Good Lord! is that all a duel amounts to! Julien thought" (p. 217). Nevertheless, the memory of his earlier dishonor persists, influencing his decision to accept Mathilde's proposal of an after-midnight tryst: "If I turn back, I'll despise myself forever! All my life long this action will be a matter of doubt for me, and in my case this sort of doubt is the most terrible of pains. Didn't I feel the same way about Amanda's lover? I believe I'd pardon myself more readily for an open crime" (p. 271).

Julien possesses a devotion to duty that no moralist can surpass, but he accepts none of the ethical values from which the idea of duty is generally derived. Since his concept of obligation is not based upon a coherent ego ideal, any deed, regardless of its goal, can appear to him in the guise of a duty as long as it involves an element of risk. Once he is struck by the realization that a particular action is both possible and dangerous, he will despise himself unless he undertakes it. As soon as Julien conceives of the idea of holding Mme de Rênal's hand, he is tormented by his sense of duty: "The idea of an obligation to fulfill, and of ridicule, or at least a sense of inferiority, to be endured if one did not succeed, immediately drove the last trace of pleasure from his heart'' (p. 42). No motive is more compelling to him than the fear of being a coward. Distrustful of Mathilde, he accepts an invitation to her room only because it occurs to him that his refusal would suggest a lack of courage.[27]

When honor does not rest upon culturally endorsed values, it becomes an extremely problematic concept. Stendhal never attempts to analyze Julien's notion of honor—a quality so fragile that it can be threatened not only by the rude stare of a boor but perhaps even by the kindness of a protector. Abbé Chélan's careful arrangements for Julien's departure from Verrières cause his protégé to wonder "whether his honor shouldn't take offense at all the pains that M. Chélan, who after all wasn't his father, had lavished on him" (p. 125). The dishonor that Julien fears above all else is not precisely the equivalent of shame: his remorse over his failure to fight in Besançon does not result from his having been judged a coward by anyone present. But this dishonor has even less in common with guilt since it is unrelated to moral considerations. Like Conrad's Lord Jim, Julien is determined to live up to an idea of honor that he never closely examines. Jim, who has ample opportunity to emulate his childhood heroes, lacks the necessary self-possession; Julien, however, lacking none of the daring required for heroic feats, finds himself in a world where honor involves little more than the willingness to risk one's life in senseless duels.[28]

When Julien plays the role of a hypocrite, he assumes that a total disjunction exists between the person that others take him for and the person he truly is. But when honor is at stake, his self-evaluation depends in part upon his identity in the eyes of a public whose judgment he normally despises. Thus, for example, he accounts for his determination to fight Amanda's lover with the assertion, "No one will every say I failed to resent an insult" (p. 132). Julien's ultimate goal is self-approbation, not public approval. But in order to judge his own behavior he often must adopt the vantage point of another.

The relationship between Julien's public and private identity becomes particularly interesting in the final section of the novel. Julien prides himself on his indifference to public opinion of his crime and angrily rebukes Mathilde and Fouqué for speaking to him of public rumors: "One dies as one can; I want to think about death only in my own personal way. What do *other people* matter? My relations with *other people* are going to be severed abruptly. For heaven's sake, don't talk to me of those people any more" (p. 382). But in spite of this vehement assertion of self-sufficiency, Julien does not appear wholly indifferent to fame, for he continues: "It seems that my fate is to die in a dream. An obscure creature like myself, who is sure to be forgotten in two weeks' time, would be a complete fool to play out the comedy." How much of his contempt for public opinion, we wonder, results from a fear of public indifference?

Julien has nothing but scorn for the values according to which the people of Verrières will judge him. But even though he considers himself the sole arbiter of his genuine identity, he proves far from indifferent to defamation by a publicity-hungry priest. Less disturbing to Julien than the priest's actual assertions is the fact that this despicable man is referring to him by name: "And, no doubt, every minute of the day he is repeating my name! This moment was more painful than death" (p. 396). Jean Starobinski's analysis of the significance that names have for Stendhal can perhaps explain Julien's anguish: "A name is situated symbolically at the confluence of existence 'for oneself' and existence 'for others.' It is an intimate truth and a public thing. In accepting my name I accept that there be a common denominator between my inner being and my social being . . . Confined to our name, our identity becomes alienated; it comes to us through and from others.''[29] Indifferent to public opinion as long as he assumes a total disjunction between public image and private self, Julien suddenly becomes vulnerable when he is made to feel that, by virtue of his name, the two are inextricably linked.

Fearing that he will die a coward, Julien consoles himself with the following thought: "If this morning, at the moment when death seemed so horrible to me, I had been called to execution, *the public eye would have been my spur to glory*; perhaps my step might have been a trifle heavy, like that of a timid fop entering a drawing room. And a few clairvoyant people, if there are any such in the provinces, might have been able to guess my weakness . . . but nobody *would have seen it* . . . I am a coward this very minute, but nobody will ever know it'' (p. 398). Julien appears to have come a long way since declaring his total indifference to the opinion of other people, but his ultimate concern is still self-approval. However, he now attributes to his audience the power to define the self that he will judge. At the moment of death Julien's hidden emotions will be irrelevant, for his opinion of himself will rest entirely on his appearance in the public eye.

Like the French lieutenant of Conrad's *Lord Jim*, Julien concludes that courageous action does not require an intrinsically fearless nature, but only a commitment to a sense of honor that is rooted in the eye of others. However, the notion of honor that Stendhal suggests cannot "reduce itself to not being found out,'' for the eye of others is internalized by the Stendhalian conscience, and a fear of dishonor becomes an abhorrence of dishonorable action.

When an individual rejects the values shared by those around him, he denies the validity of public opinion and hence makes himself sole judge of his identity. But his privileged position vis-à-vis his own feelings and motives can easily make unflattering facts seem irrelevant. Stendhal averts this danger by postulating a notion of honor that makes it possible to combine a purely personal moral code with objective self-evaluation. An anecdote in one of Stendhal's letters provides an interesting illustration of his perspective. The letter, signed ''Justin Louaut,'' is actually a short first-person narrative. Louaut declares that he saw a boat capsize on the Seine two days before. Hearing the drowning boatman call for help but unwilling to risk an attack of rheumatism by jumping into the water, he began to walk rapidly away.

> ''Devil take him!'' I said to myself, and set about thinking of other matters. Suddenly I said to myself: ''Lieutenant Louaut,'' (my name is Louaut) ''you are a sh-t. In a quarter of an hour this man will be drowned, and all your life long you will hear his cry for help.'' ''Sh-t! Sh-t!'' said the side of prudence, '' 'tis easy to say that. What of the sixty-seven days when rheumatism kept you in your bed last year? Devil take him! A boatman should know how to swim.'' I walked very quickly towards the École militaire. Suddenly a voice said to me: *''Lieutenant Louaut, you are a coward!''* This word startled me. ''Ah, *that* is serious!'' I said to myself, and started running towards the Seine. When I reached the bank, it took but one movement to throw off my coat, boots and trousers. I was the happiest of men. ''No, Louaut is no coward! Not a bit of it!'' I said to myself aloud. The upshot was, I saved the man, who would have drowned but for me . . .

What caused me to perform my fine action?—for "heroic" is
certainly too strong. Upon my word, it was fear of contempt. It
was that voice saying to me: *"Lieutenant Louaut, you are a
coward."* What startled me was that the voice addressed me in
the second person plural. *"Vous"* are a coward! As soon as I had
realized that I could save the poor clumsy fellow, it became my
duty to do so. Had I not jumped into the water, I would have
despised myself.[30]

Virtuous actions, Stendhal suggests, derive neither from
natural benevolence nor from a need for public approval. In
the absence of witnesses the self assumes the vantage point of
a hypothetical other to enforce a certain standard of behavior.
From a subjective point of view Louaut has no difficulty in
justifying his action. Only when he sees himself with the eye
of another does he perceive that his excuses are contemptible.
Julien Sorel seems to experience a similar split between the
judging and the acting self. "I have not *lived in isolation* on
the earth," he declares; "I had the powerful idea of *duty*"
(p. 402). For Julien, as for Louaut, duty apparently plays the
role of an external observer and guide.

THE hypocrisy that characterizes Julien's life and the stoicism
that marks his death have a good deal in common: in the interest of ambition Julien disguises feelings that would injure
his career; in the interest of honor he suppresses those that
threaten his self-esteem. In both cases he proves capable of
creating a public self by sheer force of will. André Malraux
includes Julien, along with Vautrin, Raskolnikov, and Ivan
Karamozov, in a list of literary characters who "accomplish
premeditated acts in accordance with a general conception of
life." Such characters, Malraux declares, "respond to the
profound human desire to act while governing one's
action."[31]

But although the determination with which Julien pursues his goals is our primary reason for considering him an exceptional man, to define him only in terms of his ambition is to make him a less sympathetic figure than Stendhal intended him to be. If Julien were to be judged by his acts alone, the damning letter composed by Mme de Rênal's confessor might well be accepted as a more or less accurate summary of his character. It is certainly true that he "has tried by means of the most consummate hypocrisy . . . to find himself a position and rise in the world" (p. 362). And the thought of using a woman to forward his career is by no means alien to him. When he first conceives of kissing Mme de Rênal's hand, he argues, "It will be cowardice on my part not to carry out a scheme that may be useful to me" (p. 24). Julien's motives in seducing his two mistresses are less exclusively pragmatic than the priest's letter suggests; but, at least initially, ambition certainly plays a greater part in his love-making than desire.

Few readers, however, would describe the hero of *The Red and the Black* as simply a vulgar adventurer, for Stendhal encourages us to respond not only to Julien's actions but to a quality of soul that elevates him above the events of his life. The "sensitivity" and "imagination" that Stendhal himself repeatedly "confesses" in *Henry Brulard* are probably the virtues he holds in highest esteem.[32] By endowing Julien with these characteristics Stendhal implicitly directs us to regard him with sympathy. Still partially within a tradition that had made masculine tears the sign of an inward grace, Stendhal expects us to admire Julien for his capacity to weep, whether his tears spring from gratitude, compassion, or merely overwrought nerves. Deep significance is attached to his exaltation at the sound of a cathedral bell: "Never will he make a good priest or a great administrator. Souls that can be so stirred are good, at most, to produce an artist" (p. 155). Early in the novel Stendhal goes so far as to suggest that Julien is ambitious only because "the delicacy of his heart makes absolutely necessary for him some of those pleasures that money bestows" (p. 30). But, perhaps because it is difficult to find occasions for dramatizing the sensitive feelings of a character whose first rule of conduct is to hide these feelings, Stendhal is less successful at conveying to us the delicacy of Julien's heart than the extraordinary strength of his will.

Far from openly trying to convince the reader of Julien's nobility, Stendhal is generally ironic in his explicit evaluations of his hero's behavior. But Stendhal's use of irony differs from that of most nineteenth-century novelists. A writer who is wholeheartedly committed to a particular system of values and able to assume that his audience will share his presuppositions will frequently employ irony as a witty means of expressing an unambiguous authorial judgment. Stendhal, on the other hand, uses irony to avoid committing himself to a clear-cut moral position and at the same time create the impression of a fully controlled perspective.[33] His tongue-in-cheek evaluations of Julien provide a means of handling his own ambivalence toward the traits that make this character an extraordinary man. For example, when Julien fails to hide his worldliness from Abbé Chélan, Stendhal interjects the following "defense" of his hero: "Let us not think too poorly of Julien's future; he was inventing, with perfect correctness, the language of a sly and prudent hypocrisy. At his age, that's not bad. In the matter of tone and gestures, he lived among yokels, and so had never studied the great models. Later, circumstances permitted him to approach closer to fine gentlemen; no sooner had he done so than he was as skillful with gestures as with words'' (p. 37). The tone of this passage suggests that Stendhal's ostensible praise is in fact an expression of disapproval. But, as we have seen, it is only by achieving a ''sly and prudent hypocrisy'' that Julien can make use of his talent in a world where pious conformity is required for advancement. Thus there is reason to believe that Stendhal's own attitude is conveyed no less by his literal words of approval than by the contrary judgment suggested by his ironic stance. Stendhal's elusive irony is an indispensable technique for dealing with the tension in his attitude toward Julien, a tension that stems in part from conflicting ideas about the nature of personal identity. To the extent that Stendhal equates authentic selfhood with an intrinsic, nonvolitional nature, he approves only of the ''sensitive'' Julien who acts unreflectively, governed wholly by impulse. However, Stendhal's devotion to spontaneity coexists with a deep admiration for the self-discipline that enables his ambitious protagonist to create an identity of his choice.

Stendhal's attitude is particularly ambiguous when he writes about his hero's amorous activities. It is by no means clear whether Julien's behavior as a lover is to be admired primarily as a triumph of will over impulse or of impulse over will. From his first attempt to hold her hand until his trembling entry into her bedroom, Julien's pursuit of Mme de Rênal reflects a continual victory of will over inclination. He achieves success, however, only after he loses all self-possession, falls at the angry woman's feet, and bursts into tears. Shortly thereafter Julien's will again prevails and he tries to act like a man of the world. In view of Mme de Rênal's response, we can only conclude that he is unsuccessful in what Stendhal describes as ''incredible efforts to spoil the effect of all his own charm'' (p. 69). Subsequently, while his remorse-ridden mistress struggles in vain against her passion, Julien has little reason to resist his inclinations, which are generally in perfect accord with the dictates of his will.

When Julien embarks upon his affair with Mathilde de La Mole, he is determined not to become emotionally involved: ''I should be a good deal more stupid than the situation calls for if ever I let myself be attracted into some feeling for this big blond doll'' (p. 267). In spite of his resolution, however, Julien falls in love with his employer's daughter and finds himself at the mercy of uncontrollable feelings: ''Julien had no notion of such intense misery; he was on the point of screaming aloud; this hypocritical soul, to whom hypocrisy was almost second nature, was completely overwhelmed'' (p. 286). Stendhal had previously chided Julien for trying to succeed in love by sheer effort of will. But when Julien's passion for Mathilde undermines his volition, Stendhal again criticizes his protagonist, this time pointing out that by failing to assert himself, Julien is ''leaving up to chance the disposition of his own destiny'' (p. 296).

When Julien finally wins Mathilde by carefully contriving to arouse her jealousy, Stendhal appears ambivalent toward his behavior. At one point Julien is faintly praised for having at least enough will power to carry out instructions: ''This head, usually so cool, had, as we see, sunk into a state of complete irrationality. Of all the qualities that had once distinguished him, nothing remained but a little firmness'' (p. 326). Since Stendhal usually writes of love as an exalting rather than a demeaning state, we suspect that despite the spatial metaphor used here (''*descendu*'' in the French text) to describe Julien's emotional condition, his irrational state is to be regarded with approbation rather than pity or scorn. But even if we assume that Stendhal approves of his protagonist's state of mind, it is not clear whether he is ironic in his praise of Julien's firmness or in his qualification of this praise. In his carefully executed conquest of Mathilde's heart Julien seems to be acting in accordance with the fundamental Beylistic principle of using one's energy in the interests of one's happiness.[34] But if we translate Stendhal's lukewarm praise of Julien's firmness into wholehearted approval of his strength, we may have to reconsider our conclusion several pages later. Having succeeded in reducing Mathilde to tears, Julien resists his longing to speak to her for fear of betraying his emotion. "In my opinion," the narrator comments, "this was one of the finest traits of his character; a man capable of imposing such restraint on his own impulses may go far" (p. 342). In responding with such extravagant praise to Julien's deliberate coldness, Stendhal once again uses apparent irony to disguise his own ambivalence.

ALTHOUGH Stendhal sometimes appears to judge Julien in purely Rousseauistic terms, valuing him primarily for the impulsive and sensitive nature that he cannot completely suppress, it is, in fact, largely the Byronic side of Stendhal himself—his energy, restlessness, and commitment to volitional self-creation—that he projects onto his most memorable hero. A fear of passivity is central to Julien's character. He is convinced that happiness can be found only through continual striving: "The man who's just climbed a mountain sits down at the top, and finds perfect satisfaction in resting there. Would he be just as happy if forced to rest all the time?" (p. 124).[35] Working toward a goal is more important to Julien than actually attaining it. Disgusted by the pettiness of the Besançon seminary and by his lack of success there, he contemplates leaving to teach Latin: "But then, no more

52

career, no more future for his imagination: it was death to think of'' (p. 149).

Constantly striving toward a distant goal, Julien experiences the present only as a bridge to something that lies ahead. His perpetual orientation toward a future identity exemplifies a condition that Jean Paul Sartre has declared to be universal to man: "The nature of consciousness implies . . . that it project itself into the future," Sartre writes. "We can understand what it is only through what it will be. It is determined in its present being by its own possibilities . . . And if we steep ourselves thus in the future, is not the formless brutality of the present thereby attenuated?"[36] To Stendhal, the formless brutality of the present appears in the less philosophical but equally unwelcome guise of boredom. Lucien Leuwen, who has no ambition and therefore exists entirely in an often trivial present, is frequently bored.[37] But Julien, steeped in the future, never experiences the torment of *ennui*. On the other hand, fully preoccupied with the possible consequences of his actions, he tends to be oblivious to present pleasures: for example, while making love for the first time, he can think only of the "perpetual ridicule" that would result from failure.

During most of his life Julien Sorel is so concerned with achieving the goals he has set for himself that he cannot experience ordinary joys. But earned self-approbation repeatedly provides him with an intense, albeit shortlived, happiness. Having carried out his plan of holding Mme de Rênal's hand, he credits himself with a heroic achievement: "Overjoyed at this thought, he locked himself into his room and surrendered himself with a new sort of pleasure entirely to reading of the exploits of his hero" (p. 44). Similarly, the first time he makes love to Mathilde his only pleasure derives from ego gratification: "He was surprised at not feeling the least happiness; finally, in order to feel some, he had recourse to his reason. He saw himself much admired by this girl who was so proud and who never bestowed her praises unreservedly; and this line of reasoning led him finally to a happiness founded on self-approval" (p. 276).

Whether the pleasure of gratified ambition can indeed equal that of genuine love is not a meaningful question for Julien since he has no choice but to pursue the only happiness he is capable of experiencing. "It is against his nature, it is impossible that man should not always, at any given moment, do what in that moment is possible and which gives him the most pleasure," Stendhal wrote in his treatise on love (p. 197). In suggesting that man has no choice but to pursue his own happiness, Stendhal appears to be anticipating the Utilitarian concept of self-interest that Dostoyevsky was to attack so vehemently in *Notes from the Undergound*. But Stendhal's theory of human motivation is in some ways even closer to that of the modern psychologist than Dostoyevsky's. Whereas Dostoyevsky denies that human behavior can, in fact, be explained in terms of self-interest, Stendhal redefines self-interest to include goals that do not seem conducive to happiness in any rational, predictable way. When Julien punishes himself for praising Napoleon by strapping his arm to his chest for two months, he hardly seems to exemplify a universal pursuit of pleasure. However, by undergoing this self-imposed chastisement he is able to regain the self-esteem that his moment of weakness had cost him. Self-interest as Stendhal perceives it may be totally unrelated to physical or economic well-being, for it can be defined only in terms of the emotional needs of a particular individual.

In his portrayal of the compulsively ambitious Julien, Stendhal seems to have intuited a pattern of causality codified almost a century later by Alfred Adler. Central to Adler's theory is the idea that a sense of inferiority during childhood will lead to an obsessive desire for preeminence in adult life, a desire that "transforms the relation of the individual to his environment into hostility and . . . drives an individual towards a goal either along a direct path such as aggressiveness or along byways suggested by precaution." The victim of an inferiority complex will pursue his chosen object with total dedication, all his actions dominated by "an imagined terminal goal."[38] Despised by his family, invariably beaten in public games, Julien as a child compensates for his weakness through identification with symbols of rebellious courage. Stendhal explicitly links Julien's admiration for his first mentor to his own sense of inferiority: "Scorned by everyone as a weakling, Julien had worshipped that old surgeon-major who one day dared to address the mayor on the subject of the plane trees" (p. 14). The surgeon-major introduces Julien to Rousseau and Napoleon, who become his new idols. Julien's identification with Napoleon is thus not the sole cause of his dreams of glory, as is sometimes assumed, but rather a channel for a preexisting emotional need.

Among the long-term effects of Julien's early humiliations is a hypersensitive pride that places him continually on the defensive. Although the possession of a phenomenal memory that brings him public acclaim helps convince him he is a man of superior worth, he nevertheless continues to believe that others despise him. Since nothing in his new self-image can account for the scorn he imagines, Julien attributes it to his plebeian birth. Mme de Rênal has always treated him with the greatest respect, yet he immediately ascribes a sudden coolness on her part (the result of religious scruples) to the discrepancy between their social positions. Later he assumes that Mathilde de La Mole will be reluctant to face the fact that her lover was born a peasant. "Never imagine, Mlle de La Mole, that I am going to forget my social position," he reflects. "I will make you understand and feel that it is for the son of a carpenter that you are betraying a descendant of the famous Guy de Croisenois" (p. 262). In this case Julien's assumption that his birth will be despised reinforces his sense of personal triumph. He would undoubtedly have found his success less gratifying had he realized that his inferior social position has been instrumental in stimulating Mathilde's love.

Class prejudice undoubtedly does exist in the world Stendhal depicts, but Julien's constant expectation of being rejected prepares him time after time to defy a nonexistent scorn. Having totally misjudged public reaction to his crime, Julien is startled on the day of his trial to meet with sympathy instead of antagonism: "Julien had no feeling other than philosophic pity for this crowd of envious folk which, without any cruel intent, was about to applaud his sentencing to death. He was quite surprised when, having been held back for more than a quarter of an hour amid the crowd, he saw that his presence aroused in the public only warmth and compassion. He heard not a single disagreeable word" (p. 385).

When Julien attacks the jury during his trial, the power of his rhetoric, as well as the hatred of the provincial bourgeoisie that Stendhal has instilled in us, inclines us to believe every word of his diatribe even though we may question the motive for his impolitic outburst. Julien declares, "I see before me men who, without ever considering whether my youth merits some pity, are determined to punish in me and discourage forever a certain class of young men—those who, born to a lower social order, and buried by poverty, are lucky enough to get a good education and bold enough to mingle with what the arrogant rich call good society. There is my crime, gentlemen'' (pp. 387-388). It is by no means clear, however, that the jury was determined to find Julien guilty before he delivered this speech. Valenod, who is something of a *parvenu* himself, is the one member of the jury unquestionably determined to see Julien convicted. But in view of Valenod's vain attempts to win Mme de Rênal's favors, his hatred of Julien would appear to have a more personal basis than commitment to the status quo. Julien has just been forced to recognize that, contrary to his assumptions, most of those present at his trial, as well as the crowd waiting outside, are warmly sympathetic to him. Of all the people in Besançon, including many members of the bourgeoisie, why should the jury alone be determined that he die? It is not surprising, of course, that Julien's accusations are supported by the outcome of his trial, for his is a self-fulfilling prophecy. By assuring the jury that they despise him Julien guarantees that they will, thereby forcing them to validate his image of himself as a heroic rebel at war with his society rather than simply an angry man who committed a senseless crime.

JULIEN'S overriding need for assurance of his worth gives him exceptional strength of will but not genuine freedom of choice. The very energy that frees him from an identity imposed by his birth also binds him to a particular way of life: ''What made Julien a superior being was precisely the quality that prevented him from seizing a pleasure that lay directly in his path'' (p. 69). During his initial affair with Mme de Rênal, his mistress's love, which is a present reality rather than a future reward, cannot satisfy Julien's constant need to strive toward a distant goal. But Mathilde de La Mole, who cannot be won without a struggle, fully occupies Julien's imagination: ''To think of something unrelated to Mlle de La Mole was beyond his power. In earlier days ambition and the simple triumphs of vanity had distracted him from the feelings that Mme de Rênal aroused in him. Mathilde had absorbed everything; he found her everywhere in his future'' (p. 316).

When Mathilde's love is finally won, it brings the unexpected bonus of a title and a commission in the hussars. Julien's response upon learning of his promotion is narrated in a puzzling manner; ''That evening, when [Mathilde] told Julien he was a lieutenant of hussars, his joy knew no bounds. It can be estimated from the ambition of his whole life, and from the passion he was now feeling for his new son. The change of name struck him with wonder. Now at last, he thought, the novel of my career is over, and the credit is all mine. I was able to make myself loved by that monster of pride, he thought, glancing at Mathilde; her father cannot live without her nor she without me'' (p. 359).

There is a striking discrepancy between what Stendhal tells and what he shows. We are assured that Julien is filled with joy, wonder, and paternal love, but when his actual thoughts are transcribed, they reflect a far less positive state of mind. Stendhal appears to be torn between two conflicting views of his protagonist. While the commentator tries to fit Julien into a conventional mold, the dramatist intuitively senses what such a man's true emotions would be. Julien immediately perceives his commission not as the beginning but as the end of his career. His arrogant claim that he alone deserves credit for this appointment suggests a need to compensate for the realization that his future is no longer in his own hands. Julien has never been blind to Mathilde's faults, but at no other time does he regard her with such hatred. Having longed for a splendid career less for its intrinsic pleasures than as a means of convincing himself of his worth, he is understandably ambivalent toward a promotion that he owes more to fertility than to talent. Furthermore, the achievement of his ostensible goal leaves him nothing further to strive for. Notwithstanding his grim boast, Julien is well aware that from now on his fate will rest upon the whims of his imperious wife and her doting father. His pride forces him to despise his benefactors so that instead of having to acknowledge his dependence, he can perceive them as mere tools of his will.

As the contradictions within this passage indicate, Stendhal's dramatic portrayal of Julien is not always congruent with his explicit analysis of this character. Values that Stendhal inherited from his Romantic forebears apparently led him to conceive of his hero as a young man who combines a generous, affectionate nature with extraordinary strength of will. But Stendhal's actual portrayal of Julien calls into question the very dichotomy upon which it seems to rest. Julien's behavior can thus be more convincingly explained in the language of Freud and Adler than that of Byron and Rousseau.

If the novel of Julien's career ends when he acquires a title and commission, the last fifty pages of *The Red and the Black* certainly constitute one of the most interesting appendices in literary history. Julien's shooting of Mme de Rênal, which occupies only a page of text from conception to execution, has occasioned much critical controversy. Usually so thorough in analyzing the motives of his heroes' behavior, Stendhal provides no clue to the thoughts and emotions that lead to this crime. Julien presumably reaches his fatal resolution immediately upon reading Mme de Rênal's letter. During this one scene Stendhal modifies his narrative method, denying us our accustomed access to Julien's consciousness. The familiar omniscient narrator accompanies Julien from Strasbourg to Paris, telling us of Julien's "frightful doubts." This narrator next appears on the journey from Paris to Verrières, when he informs us of Julien's intention of writing to Mathilde. But during Julien's brief stop in Paris, authorial presence is reflected only in a remark about Mme de Rênal's handwriting. Deprived of our privileged view of Julien's hidden feelings, we see him at this crucial moment only through a camera's eye.[39]

Our first impression of Julien's crime may suggest that for once in his life he succumbs to a passion that overwhelms his self-control. His previous behavior has led us to identify his will with his ambition. Since his attack upon Mme de Rênal implies a total disregard for his own future, it appears to represent a victory of impulse over volition. But it has been clear since the beginning of the novel that Julien values honor even above professional advancement. He was ready to refuse M. de Rênal's attractive offer of employment to avoid the humiliation of eating with servants; he would have sacrificed his future in the church rather than refuse to fight in a Besançon café; and after arriving in Paris he risked his life in a duel because he thought himself insulted. When his honor is attacked by Mme de Rênal's letter, his sense of duty demands that he seek revenge.

The meager knowledge that we have of Julien's behavior upon reading Mme de Rênal's letter suggests that his departure for Verrières is marked by firm determination rather than violent anger. "I cannot blame M. de La Mole, Julien said, when he had finished it; he is perfectly right and proper. What father would want to give his beloved daughter to such a man! Farewell!" (p. 362). Only after Julien has resolved upon his course of action does he lose his self-possession to such an extent that he is unable to write. But the power of Julien's will has never extended over his limbs. Early in his career, having resolved to seduce Mme de Rênal, he trembled so violently on his way to her room that he had to lean against a wall. Julien's decision to kill the woman who has blackened his name is less inconsistent with what we know of his nature than it first appears to be. There is reason to believe, in fact, that he regards shooting his former mistress as a duty every bit as compelling, though even more distasteful, than seducing her had once been.[40] Julien must make a tremendous effort of will to execute his resolution: "The sight of this woman whom he had loved deeply made Julien's arm tremble so violently that at first he could not carry out his plan. I cannot do it, he told himself; physically, I cannot do it" (p. 363). Only when Mme de Rênal's face is hidden from his view is he able to fire. After he has been imprisoned, Julien reaffirms the principles upon which he has acted: "I have been insulted in atrocious fashion; I have killed, I have deserved death myself, but that's all. I die after settling my score with humanity" (p. 365). Julien's attack upon the woman he once loved is in a sense the ultimate proof of his strength of will. But the fact that he perceives this crime to be dictated by duty does not mean that his behavior can be wholly explained in terms of his conscious values.

His decision to avenge his honor by this self-destructive act becomes easier to understand if we bear in mind his strange bitterness upon first hearing of his lieutenancy. As we have seen, Julien believed the "novel" of his career to have ended with his military appointment, which marked the conclusion of his struggle for success and wrested his future out of his hands. Once he joins his company, his faith in his power of self-determination temporarily returns, and he begins to dream about becoming commander-in-chief. But Mathilde's letter interrupts his dreams and rudely reminds him how little control he now has over his fate. "All is lost . . . come as quickly as possible, give up everything, desert if need be" (p. 361), writes Mathilde in her usual imperious tone, and Julien has no choice but to obey at once. Had Julien simply left matters in his mistress's hands, it is quite possible that Mathilde, apparently undaunted by what she has learned of her lover's past, could have found some way of handling her father's anger. But Julien, who dreads nothing more than inaction, has undoubtedly had his fill of waiting patiently for Mathilde and her father to settle his fate. His immediate conviction that it is incumbent upon him to shoot his detractor may result in part from an overwhelming need to do something—anything—rather than once again stand aside while Mathilde mollifies the infuriated marquis. Violence gives Julien a sense of controlling his own destiny and simultaneously provides an escape from an existence rendered meaningless by the achievement of its goal.

The fact that Julien's shooting of Mme de Rênal closely parallels a crime actually committed by a young man named Antoine Berthet may explain why Stendhal makes no attempt to defend the plausibility of so irrational an act. However, in transforming the pathetic Berthet, who shoots his former mistress while in a state of despair over repeated failure, into a character of extraordinary ability and strength of will on the verge of achieving his life's goal, Stendhal depicts a crime no less credible than Berthet's, but fundamentally different in its motives.[41]

The "gloomy energy" that motivated Julien's social rise extinguishes itself in the act of violence that irrevocably ends his career. Thereafter his emotional needs abruptly change, and he finds complete happiness in a prison cell. Stendhal seems to suggest that through his new-found love of Mme de Rênal Julien at last fulfills a formerly unrealized nature.[42] But the fact that Julien finally proves capable of genuine love for Mme de Rênal is perhaps less significant than the fact that he can experience such love only in prison, while awaiting death. A man who fears nothing more than being forced to rest all the time will never consciously choose to renounce ambition and live only for the present. Julien's psychological makeup prevents him from discovering the delights of a peaceful love until circumstances forcibly release him from his driving will.

Experiencing in prison an unprecedented joy, Julien regrets his former inability to live wholly in the present: "When I could have been so happy during our walks through the forest at Vergy, smoldering ambition dragged my soul away into imaginary lands. When I should have been pressing to my heart this lovely form that was so close to my lips, I was stolen away from you by the future" (p. 405). But notwithstanding his assertion that he is now "living from day to day" (p. 406), Julien never really learns to accept time as a continual succession of present moments. He can temporarily live in the present only because he knows there will be no future. The anticipation of death is as fundamental to his current peace as the hope of advancement was to his former energy.[43] Throughout Julien's life the struggle toward a goal had defined the meaning of his existence. When this meaning is lost, even his discovery of the joy of perfect love cannot restore his will to live. His behavior during his trial virtually guarantees a verdict of guilty. Refusing to appeal his conviction, he forbids any attempt to save his life. There can thus be little doubt that he dies by his own choice.

IN Stendhal's fiction, as in his life, a high esteem for determination, shrewd intelligence, and aggressive self-assertion coexists with a celebration of reverie and tender emotion, a scorn for prudence and ambition, an ascetic indifference to worldly rewards. The former values appear to be more fundamental to him, but they are also the source of considerable ambivalence, and it is generally to the latter that he gives his conscious assent. Thus it is only in the final section of *The*

Red and the Black, when Julien has renounced all ambition, that Stendhal suspends his characteristic irony and encourages us to view his protagonist with unqualified approbation.

Able to envision no arena except a corrupt social world for the driving energy of the exceptional man, Stendhal suggests that life offers only two alternatives: a struggle for volitional self-creation that necessarily involves hypocrisy and callousness or a passive acquiescence to impulse that requires an abdication of the will. Stendhal portrays Julien as a man too sensitive to devote his life to contriving for worldly success yet too restless to find lasting happiness in passivity. (However genuine Julien's love for Mme de Rênal may be, one wonders how long his passion would survive the absence of all impediments.) The impossibility of combining energetic action with enduring affection in the world that this novel depicts precludes any resolution short of Julien's death.

2

D. H. Lawrence

The Romantic attitude toward the self had relatively little impact upon the mainstream of nineteenth-century English fiction, for the traditional English novel is concerned with personal identity primarily as a social rather than an absolute entity. Although Victorian novelists vigorously criticized the realities of their society, they were generally committed to the values it espoused. Unlike many of their Romantic predecessors, who assumed that self-fulfillment required a repudiation of societal expectations, they tended implicitly to equate true self-fulfillment with the realization of a socially sanctioned ideal.[1]

Early in the twentieth century British fiction began to challenge the moral and psychological assumptions upon which the conventional novel had rested. Joseph Conrad questioned man's capacity to triumph over the part of his being that runs counter to moral laws; James Joyce insisted that the artist must free himself from the demands of family, country, and church in the interest of his craft. However, Conrad never doubted that man should do all in his power to keep faith with "the community of mankind," and Joyce's Stephen Dedalus repudiated society's demands only to place himself in the services of art, an even more exacting master. But

D. H. Lawrence, offering a still more radical challenge to Victorian assumptions, insisted that each individual's primary goal should be the fulfillment of his own impulsive nature.

Lawrence has a great deal in common with the Stendhal who prized spontaneous, unpredictable behavior—the novelist who wrote with obvious approval that Julien Sorel was "capable of the unexpected," that Lucien Leuwen was "absolutely incapable of dissimulating any change of mood, and never was there a nature more fundamentally changeable," that the conduct of the Duchessa Sanseverina was "incalculable, even by herself." On the other hand, no one could be further from sharing Lawrence's point of view than the Stendhal who declared, "We are what we succeed in being, but we are conscious of what we are."[2] The belief that man's true identity is both impervious to willed modification and inaccessible to conscious definition is the keystone of Lawrentian thought.

According to Lawrence, personal identity derives from the unconscious, which he defines as "the active, self-evolving soul bringing forth its own incarnation and self-manifestation." Individuality, "the knowledge that *I am I*," is "established physically and psychically the moment the two parent nuclei fused, at the moment of the conception."[3] But although the self is brought into being by a biological process, it is by no means simply a product of heredity: "The nature of the infant is *not* just a new permutation-and-combination of elements contained in the natures of the parents. There is in the nature of the infant that which is utterly unknown in the natures of the parents. Something which could never be derived from the natures of all the existent individuals or previous individuals. There is in the nature of the infant something entirely new, underived, underivable, something which is, and which will forever remain, *causeless*."[4]

Lawrence is more explicit than Nietzsche in defining the source of selfhood. But he shares Nietzsche's conviction that being what one truly is leads not to self-consistency but to ceaseless change. Lawrence defines character as "the flame of a man, which burns brighter or dimmer, bluer or yellower or redder, rising or sinking or flaring according to the draughts of circumstance and the changing air of life, changing itself continually, yet remaining one single, separate flame." "Creative life," he declares, "is characterized by spontaneous mutability: it brings forth unknown issues, impossible to preconceive."[5] Lawrence also parallels Nietzsche in his insistence that the intrinsic self is not necessarily a determinant of our behavior. Paradoxically, it may be easier to live an inauthentic life than to transcend one's habitual mode of existence and become what one inherently is: "a living man must leap away from himself into the . . . fires of creation . . . We must *choose* life, for life will never compel us."[6] But Lawrence's doctrine has a quasi-religious component totally lacking in Nietzsche's. Without adhering to any established religion, Lawrence vehemently opposes the notion of human self-sufficiency: "At no moment can man create himself. He can but submit to the creator, to the primal unknown out of which issues the all. At every moment we issue like a balanced flame from the primal unknown. We are not self-contained or self-accomplished."[7] Nothing could be further from Lawrence's view than the Existential conception of man as the product of his freely chosen acts. To fulfill the innate identity that Lawrence attributes to us, we must obey the will of our "creator," as expressed through our own deepest desires.

Psychoanalysis attempts to free the individual from the domination of his unconscious wishes by bringing them within the jurisdiction of his conscious will. But according to

Lawrence man must free himself not from his impulses but from the restrictive ego ideal that stifles the irrational side of his nature. Lawrence takes for granted man's capacity to choose whether to assert his conscious will or submit to his deepest longings: "So much free will there is. There is the free will to choose between submitting the will, and so becoming a spark in a great tendency, or withholding the will, curling up within the will, and so remaining outside, exempt from life or death." Instead of trying to control the course of our lives Lawrence would have us give free rein to our impulses, wherever they may lead: "This is peace like a river. This is peace like a river to flow upon the tide of the creative direction, towards an end we know nothing of, but which only fills us with bliss of confidence . . . All the while we are but given to the stream, we are borne upon the surpassing impulse which has our end in view beyond us."[8]

The orthodox Freudian has a heyday with Lawrence's biography and novels but probably dismisses his theoretical writings as the naive misconceptions of a layman. In recent years, however, a number of psychologists, attempting to reconcile Freudian and Existential doctrines, have reached conclusions strikingly similar to Lawrence's. The writings of such men as Abraham Maslow, Carl Rogers, and Rollo May recapitulate the Lawrentian theory that every individual possesses an intrinsic self, that this self is not static but continually evolving, and that the individual is free to choose whether he will suppress or realize an identity that is inherently his (see appendix).

The assumption that genuine selfhood can only be achieved by fulfilling one's intrinsic nature logically leads to moral relativism, as Lawrence himself makes clear: "There is not and cannot be any actual norm of human conduct. All depends, first, on the unknown inward need within the very nuclear centres of the individual himself, and secondly on his circumstance. Some men *must* be too spiritual, some *must* be too sensual. Some *must* be too sympathetic, and some *must* be too proud.''⁹ In his ''Study of Thomas Hardy'' Lawrence seems to argue for a nonjudgmental acceptance of all human beings: ''The hardest thing for any man to do is for him to recognize and to know that the natural law of his neighbour is other than, and maybe even hostile to, his own natural law, and yet is true.''¹⁰ Lawrence's real quarrel in this essay, however, is not with value judgments per se but with an arbitrary moral code devised by human society, which he seeks to replace by a more meaningful set of values derived from nature: ''The vast, unexplored morality of life itself, what we call the immorality of nature, surrounds us in its eternal incomprehensibility, and in its midst goes on the little human morality play'' (p. 419). It is clear throughout Lawrence's discussion of Hardy's novels that his acknowledgment of the ''eternal incomprehensibility'' of nature by no means prevents him from judging one mode of existence as intrinsically superior to another. ''The glory of mankind,'' he goes so far as to declare, ''is not in a host of secure, comfortable, law-abiding citizens, but in the few more fine, clear lives, beings, individuals, distinct, detached, single as may be from the public'' (p. 436).

Moral relativism is an attractive doctrine to Lawrence insofar as it undermines conventional values, but he is much too strongly committed to his own beliefs to maintain a consistently relativistic stance. The conflict between his theoretical acceptance of relativism and his fervent commitment to what he considers the morality of life itself is strikingly reflected in his treatment of Sue Bridehead, the female protagonist of Hardy's *Jude the Obscure*. Lawrence's lengthy discussion of this character provides considerable evidence of the intensely negative response we would expect him to have to such a woman: "One of the supremest products of our civilization is Sue, and a product that well frightens us . . . The suppressed, atrophied female in her, like a potent fury, was always there, suggesting to her to make the fatal mistake. She contained always the rarest, most deadly anarchy in her own being" (p. 497). But at the end of his analysis Lawrence suddenly shifts from his condemnation of the cerebral, asexual, self-destructive modern woman epitomized by Sue to an explicit attack upon Jude—and upon us as well—for our failure to appreciate Sue's particular kind of beauty:

> Sue had a being, special and beautiful. Why must not Jude recognize it in all its speciality? Why must man be so utterly irreverent, that he approaches each being as if it were no-being? Why must it be assumed that Sue is an "ordinary" woman—as if such a thing existed? Why must she feel ashamed if she is specialized? And why must Jude, owing to the conception he is brought up in, force her to act as if she were his "ordinary" abstraction, a woman?
>
> She was not a woman. She was Sue Bridehead, something very particular. Why was there no place for her? Cassandra had the Temple of Apollo. Why are we so foul that we have no reverence for that which we are and for that which is amongst us? (P. 510)

Lawrence repeatedly espouses a relativistic position in his theoretical writings. "Damn all absolutes," he writes in an essay called "The Novel." "Oh damn, damn, damn all absolutes . . . Everything is relative. Every Commandment that ever issued out of the mouth of God or man, is strictly relative: adhering to the particular time, place and circumstance."[11] But in "Morality and the Novel" he condemns not only the conventionally moralistic novel, whose author "puts his thumb in the pan, for love, tenderness, sweetness, peace,'' but also the ''smart and smudgily cynical novel, which says it doesn't matter what you do, because one thing is as good as another.''[12] Attacking a tradition that has raised a single emotion—love—to the status of an absolute, Lawrence argues that the novel must portray ''true and vivid relationships'' in all their ever-changing fluidity without forcing them into a preconceived pattern. The immorality of most fiction lies, he declares, in the author's blindness to his own assumptions, his ''helpless, unconscious predilection'' (p. 529). But Lawrence's own desideratum for the novel is by no means devoid of all tacit value judgments. When he writes, ''The only morality is to have man true to his manhood, woman to her womanhood, and let the relationship form of itself'' (p. 531), Lawrence may well assume that, consistent with his avowed relativism, he is demanding only that every individual be what he truly is. But the wording of this statement makes it clear that Lawrence implicitly regards fidelity to a sexual identity as an imperative that transcends all arbitrary values, having been ordained by nature as a universal law.

Lawrence opposes the concept of an absolute code of values largely because it has traditionally led to conclusions incompatible with his own. In Lawrence's vocabulary the word ''absolute'' refers to conventional rules of conduct: the values he upholds are identified not with morality, but with life. When an individual transgresses against Lawrentian values, he is accused not of evil, but of nullity, decay, putrescence. We need only remind ourselves of Lawrence's treatment of such characters as Hermione and Loerke in *Women in Love,* Carlota in *The Plumed Serpent*, or Sir Clifford in *Lady Chatterley's Lover* to perceive the unbreachable gap between genuine relativism and Lawrence's quasi-religious commitment to a particular view of life.

Conventional moral judgments have traditionally rested on the assumption that man has the power and responsibility to choose his actions. As Conrad's *Lord Jim* suggests, such judgments have been rendered problematic by the realization that human behavior is sometimes the product of unconscious forces the individual is powerless to control. For Lawrence, however, the question of conscious volition has no bearing on moral judgment: "And why a man should be held guilty of his conscious intentions, and innocent of his unconscious intentions, I don't know, since every man is more made up of unconscious intentions than of conscious ones. I am what I am, not merely what I think I am."[13]

Since Lawrentian doctrine forbids any attempt to resist a natural impulse, Lawrence must either refrain from judging individuals on any basis except authenticity or else he must judge them by their intrinsic nature. Embracing the latter of these alternatives, Lawrence becomes the proponent of a kind of secularized Calvinism. The terms in which he couches what he takes to be Whitman's message of American democracy reflect the quasi-religious quality of his own doctrine. The soul, he maintains, "is known at once in its going . . . Not by works at all. Not by anything, but just itself."[14] The man to whom grace has been granted will know he is among the elect: "If a man feels superior, he should have it out with himself. 'Do I feel superior because I *am* superior? Or is it just the snobbishness of class, or education, or money?' Class, education, money won't make a man superior. But if he's just *born* superior, in himself, there it is. Why deny it?"[15]

This piece of advice is hardly one we would expect from an inveterate enemy of the self-conscious ego. But self-consciousness, like moral relativism, plays an extremely problematic role in Lawrence's writing. He frequently argues that one's true identity is inaccessible to conscious thought. Self-definitions are static, he declares, but a man's genuine self is continually changing: "In all this change, I maintain a certain integrity. But woe betide me if I try to put my finger on it. If I say of myself, I am this, I am that!—then, if I stick to it, I turn into a stupid fixed thing like a lamp-post. I shall never know wherein lies my integrity, my individuality, my me."[16] An individual's attempt to define his identity, Lawrence suggests, can only lead to an arbitrary limitation of his potentialities and thus prevent genuine self-realization. But elsewhere Lawrence stresses the importance of trying to understand one's own nature. In his foreword to *Women in Love* he argues in favor of conceptualizing emotional experiences: "Man struggles with his unborn needs and fulfillment. New unfoldings struggle up in torment in him, as buds struggle forth from the midst of a plant. Any man of real individuality tries to know and to understand what is happening, even in himself, as he goes along. This struggle for verbal consciousness should not be left out in art. It is a very great part of life."[17]

Although, as Frederick J. Hoffman has observed, Lawrence attacks Freud for bringing into consciousness what Lawrence thinks is better left unconscious,[18] he also warns against failing to acknowledge those aspects of our psyche that we find unacceptable: "If there is a serpent of secret and shameful desire in my soul, let me not beat it out of my consciousness with sticks. It will lie beyond, in the marsh of the so-called subconsciousness, where I cannot follow it with my sticks. Let me bring it to the fire to see what it is."[19] Furthermore, despite his well-known hostility toward what he calls "sex in the head," Lawrence argues in "A Propos of *Lady Chatter-ley's Lover*" that only conscious awareness can prevent the sex act from becoming mechanical:

> Today the full conscious realization of sex is even more important than the act itself. After centuries of obfuscation, the mind demands to know and know fully . . . our ancestors have so assiduously acted sex without ever thinking it or realizing it, that now the act tends to be mechanical, dull and disappointing, and only fresh mental realization will freshen up the experience.
>
> The mind has to catch up, in sex: indeed, in all the physical acts. Mentally, we lag behind in our sexual thought, in a dimness, a lurking, grovelling fear which belongs to our raw, somewhat bestial ancestors. In this one respect, sexual and physical, we have left the mind unevolved. Now we have to catch up, and make a balance between the consciousness of the body's sensations and experiences, and these sensations and experiences themselves.[20]

Although Lawrence believes it is impossible to achieve an authentic identity by striving to fulfill a conscious conception of oneself, he nevertheless hopes to modify his readers' lives by changing their conscious notions of what they do in fact feel: "My field is to know the feelings inside a man, and to make new feelings conscious. What really torments civilized people is that they are full of feelings they know nothing about; they can't realize them, they can't fulfill them, they can't *live* them." Lawrence acknowledges, moreover, that self-knowledge, though not to be valued as an end in itself, is a prerequisite to self-realization: "You've got to know yourself as far as possible. But not just for the sake of knowing. You've got to know yourself so that you can at last *be* yourself."[21] But if self-knowledge must precede self-realization, an individual can become himself only after he has formulated a conscious conception of his nature. Lawrence contradicts himself on this matter because it is not really self-awareness per se that he is judging. He detests self-analysis based on a rationalistic theory of the human psyche, but he advocates efforts to understand one's actual feelings and desires. The difference between these two processes perhaps lies less in their methods than in their conclusions: accurate self-knowledge, unlike arbitrary self-definition, is presumably that which provides a true (that is, Lawrentian) conception of one's deepest nature.

If, as Lawrence sometimes suggests, mental consciousness can only lead to the suppression of genuine impulses, his own goal as a writer is unattainable, for his books will merely provide one more pattern for the conscious ego to imitate. Only if a salutary connection can exist between our minds and our feelings, if consciousness can reveal our genuine nature to us, if understanding our emotions can help us to experience them is Lawrence justified in assuming that the novel has the power to "present us with new, really new feelings, a whole line of new emotion, which will get us out of the emotional rut."[22]

The need to move beyond established convention in pursuit of a new way of life is a dominant theme in Lawrence's major works. His novels repeatedly portray characters striving to free themselves from the restrictions that their family and society attempt to impose upon them. When they repudiate societal demands, they do so with their creator's blessings. Although the opening section of *The Rainbow* celebrates an age when authentic selfhood was compatible with social integration, both the conclusion of this novel and the whole of *Women in Love* suggest that modern man must break away from inherited values in his pursuit of self-realization. But during the latter part of his life Lawrence became increasingly pessimistic about the efficacy of individualistic rebellion. In *Studies in Classic American Literature* he goes so far as to insist that true fulfillment can be achieved only within the framework of a traditional way of life: "Men are free when they are in a living homeland, not when they are straying and breaking away. Men are free when they are obeying some deep, inward voice of religious belief. Obeying from within. Men are free when they belong to a living, organic, *believing* community . . . Men are freest when they are most unconscious of freedom."[23]

As Stendhal observed, patterns of behavior learned in earliest childhood become almost indistinguishable from instincts. Stable communities whose unchanging values have been passed down through generations thus provide a mode of existence that may well seem to be ordained by nature. In rebelling against an established way of life, men and women elevate conscious volition over habits so deeply ingrained that they appear inborn. Thus the same commitment to instinct that had once made Lawrence an opponent of all convention now leads him to embrace tradition as a bulwark against the iconoclastic, power-hungry will.

During the latter part of his career Lawrence comes to doubt not only man's ability to fulfill his nature by rebelling against the social order, but also his capacity to distinguish his true desires from values his society has taught him. In *The Plumed Serpent* Cipriano declares that Kate cannot possibly discover her real nature through introspection alone because her perceptions are corrupted by her culture:

> You think like a modern woman, because you belong to the Anglo-Saxon or Teutonic world, and dress your hair in a certain way, and have money, and are altogether free.—But you only think like this because you have had these thoughts put in your

head, just as in Mexico you spend centavos and pesos, because that is the Mexican money you have put in your pocket. It's what they give you at the bank.—So when you say you are free, you are *not* free. You are compelled all the time to be thinking U.S.A. thoughts—*compelled*, I must say. You have not as much choice as a slave. As the peons must eat tortillas, tortillas, tortillas, because there is nothing else, you must think these U.S.A. thoughts, about being a woman and being free.[24]

This assertion calls into question a great deal of what Lawrence has written elsewhere, for it suggests that cultural conditioning may in fact preclude the realization of a purely instinctual self. But instead of facing the full implications of this statement, Lawrence attributes such conditioning to only a particular kind of social world, suggesting that Ramón and Cipriano, free of all distorting biases, are not only in touch with their own true nature but aware of Kate's as well. In a late essay, however, Lawrence carries Cipriano's argument to its logical conclusion, maintaining that all human characteristics are socially determined: "When Oscar Wilde said that it was nonsense to assert that art imitates nature, because nature always imitates art, this was absolutely true of human nature. The thing called 'spontaneous human nature' does not exist, and never did. Human nature is always made to some pattern or other . . . No man has 'feelings of his own.' The feelings of all men in the civilized world today are practically all alike. Men *can* only feel the feelings they know how to feel. The feelings they don't know how to feel, they don't feel."[25]

THE traditional novel, primarily concerned with relationships among individuals within a social framework, tends to portray its characters largely in terms of personality traits manifested through interactions with others. But the Romantic writer in search of an absolute self has little interest in an identity that derives from social intercourse. Thus Lawrence scornfully dismisses the public self as merely a "person"—that is, "a human being *as he appears to others*," and the identity it achieves as mere "personality"—"that which is transmitted from the person to his audience."[26]

Lawrence's insistence that internal, subjective states are a more essential aspect of personal identity than outwardly visible characteristics places him in the mainstream of the modern novel. However, he rejects not only the traditional novelist's goal of depicting "personality," but also the techniques of stream-of-consciousness fiction, which he views as simply another means for defining a static, knowable self: "Through thousands and thousands of pages Mr. Joyce and Miss Richardson tear themselves to pieces, strip their smallest emotions to the finest threads . . . Absorbedly, childishly concerned with *what I am*. 'I am this, I am that, I am the other. My reactions are such, and such, and such.' "[27] The portrayal of individual identity as Lawrence conceives of it—elusive, ever changing, and far more accurately revealed in unconscious impulses and physical sensations than in self-conscious analysis of one's behavior—requires a mode of characterization significantly different from that of either his predecessors or his contemporaries.

Lawrence's most frequently cited discussion of his own approach to character concerns his rejection of "the old stable ego" in favor of a new concept of the self:

I don't so much care about what the woman *feels*—in the ordinary usage of the word. That presumes an *ego* to feel with. I only care about what the woman is— what she IS—inhumanly, physiologically, materially—according to the use of the word:

but for me, what she *is* as a phenomenon (or as representing some greater, inhuman will), instead of what she feels according to the human conception. That is where the futurists are stupid. Instead of looking for the new human phenomenon, they will only look for the phenomena of the science of physics to be found in human beings . . . You mustn't look in my novel for the old stable *ego* of the character. There is another *ego*, according to whose action the individual is unrecognisable, and passes through, as it were, allotropic states which it needs a deeper sense than any we've been used to exercise, to discover are states of the same single radically unchanged element. (Like as diamond and coal are the same pure single element of carbon. The ordinary novel would trace the history of the diamond—but I say, "Diamond, what! This is carbon." And my diamond might be coal or soot, and my theme is carbon.)[28]

The precise meaning of this passage is far from clear. The dichotomy between matter and spirit central to traditional Western thought still largely governs our conceptual categories, and Lawrence's attempt to depart from a dualistic view of man's nature meets resistance from the conservatism inherent in language itself.[29] Interpreted literally, parts of Lawrence's letter to Garnett might well suggest a new book on female anatomy. To convey his repudiation of the traditional concern with the spiritual or psychological, Lawrence claims an interest in what Western culture views as the only alternative—the physiological or material. The nature of our language demands that the self be described—and, in fact, conceptualized—as either spirit or machine. When Lawrence attempts to challenge this fundamental dichotomy, he can suggest his meaning only by a paradox: he claims to be interested in what a woman is "physiologically, materially" and at the same time attacks the futurists for perceiving individuals simply as physical objects. Lawrence also claims to have no interest in a woman's feelings "in the ordinary usage of the word" or "according to the human conception." But our language does not provide a more accurate term for the intense internal states, simultaneously mental and physical, that Lawrence strives to portray. Elsewhere Lawrence himself used the word "feelings" to identify these states, insisting, for example, in a passage quoted above, that the novel must present us with "really new feelings, a whole line of new emotion."

A number of commentators on modern fiction have suggested that in repudiating the novelist's traditional task of depicting personalities modern writers have chosen to deal with the universals of human experience rather than with the individuality of particular human beings. According to Nathalie Sarraute, for example, the most significant feature of the modern novel is that "the watertight partitions that used to separate the characters from one another give way, and the hero become[s] an arbitrary limitation, a conventional figure cut from the common woof that each of us contains in its entirety." Similarly Erich Auerbach finds in modern literature a preoccupation with "the elementary things which men in general have in common."[30] But when Lawrence rejects the "old stable ego" of character, he is not denying the importance of individual identity but seeking, rather, to replace the traditional idea of a consistent self with "another ego" whose continually fluctuating states are composed of a "single, radically unchanged element" upon which selfhood rests.

Lawrence's analogy between the changing nature of the self and the allotropic forms assumed by chemical elements can easily lead to confusion, since it seems to deny significant differences among individuals. Under a certain set of conditions any lump of coal will become a diamond. But Lawrence does not mean to imply that all human beings share a com-

mon psychological makeup. That individuals differ significantly from one another is, in fact, a cornerstone of his creed:
"Each human self is single, incommutable, and unique. This
is its *first* reality."[31] His definition of selfhood requires
Lawrence to conceive of each of his characters not as a config-
uration of relatively stable attributes, but as a particular way
of responding to life. A character's intrinsic being, as
revealed through ever-changing moods, emotions, attitudes,
and sensations, must receive far more emphasis within the
novel than the relatively stable personality traits that he ex-
hibits in the presence of others, and yet the integral selfhood
of each character must not dissolve into a continuous flux of
universally experienced interior states.

To perceive the essential identity of a Lawrentian character
one must take account of his reactions to a variety of objects,
ideas, activities, events, and people, which together reveal
his fundamental relationship to a world beyond the self.
Lawrence, like Stendhal, regards a character's internal responses to the people and events around him as evidence of
his intrinsic, nonvolitional identity, an identity totally distinct from the public self that is largely a product of his will.
But whereas Stendhal regards his protagonists' capacity for
intense emotion as prima facie evidence of an admirable
nature that raises them above other, less sensitive men, Lawrence suggests no relation between intensity of feeling and
intrinsic personal worth. His negative characters are no less
capable of emotion than his positive ones, and he sometimes
even attributes very similar feelings to extremely dissimilar
figures.

All of Lawrence's major characters experience a wide spec-
trum of interior states, but not all are equally free of the underlying self-consistency that enables us to analyze and understand the characters in more traditional novels. Although

a truly vital existence as Lawrence conceives of it requires the absence of any fixed psychological structure that would impose a pattern on one's behavior, only a few exemplary characters among the many he portrays are actually capable of the "spontaneous mutability" that he attributes to creative life.

CENTRAL to *Women in Love*, Lawrence's greatest work, is a contrast between two kinds of selfhood. Of its four protagonists, one man and one woman are capable of achieving a healthy relationship, while the other man and woman are doomed to failure. The former, not limited to a restrictive self-consistency, undergo the spontaneous flux central to Lawrence's conception of the vital self. The latter, however, are characterized by underlying psychological needs that restrict them to fixed patterns of behavior. Thus ordinary techniques of analysis can be applied to Gudrun and Gerald far more appropriately than to Ursula and Birkin.

When reading the opening pages of *Women in Love* for the first time, one is struck primarily by the similarities between the Brangwen sisters, both, as F. R. Leavis has observed, "educated, intelligent, and conscious, no longer belonging to the working class into which they were born, or to any class or context that can give life bearings or direction, or in which (say) marriage has its significant and unquestionable place."[32] But during subsequent readings of the novel it becomes possible to appreciate the skill with which Lawrence contrasts his two female protagonists, making virtually every detail in the novel's opening scene reflect their fundamentally different natures.

There is a striking difference between Gudrun's urgency at the start of the dialogue (conveyed by the use of italics) and Ursula's apparent tranquillity: " 'Ursula,' said Gudrun, 'don't you *really want* to get married?' Ursula laid her embroidery in her lap and looked up. Her face was calm and considerate. 'I don't know,' she replied. 'It depends how you mean.' " As the conversation continues, Ursula repeatedly proves able to accept uncertainty, while Gudrun, intolerant of ambiguity, wants to be "quite definite." When Gudrun does not receive a decisive answer to her question, her tone of intense concern gives way to a characteristic mask of sophistication; her subsequent remarks, the narrator informs us, are delivered "ironically" or "coolly." Gudrun's approach to marriage is markedly pragmatic: "Don't you think, anyhow, you'd be—in a better position than you are in now." The wording of her next query is particularly telling: "You don't think one needs the *experience* of having been married?" (p. 1). When she imagines her future self, it is not as a wife, but as a woman who, having reaped whatever benefits matrimony can offer, has returned to a single state. Ursula, on the other hand, who assumes that marriage will be permanent, fears that it will be "the end of experience," a state of inescapable stasis.

A short while later, the sisters talk more specifically about their reluctance to marry. Assenting to Gudrun's suggestion that marriage seems to be "the inevitable next step," Ursula continues, "But really imagine it: imagine any man one knows, imagine him coming home to one every evening, and saying 'Hello', and giving one a kiss—." "Yes," Gudrun replies, "It's just impossible. The man makes it impossible" (p. 3). While Ursula's description of conventional domesticity reinforces our impression that the primary cause of her reluctance to marry is a fear of unchanging routine, Gudrun's vehement response involves a telling shift of focus. Her statement suggests that her dread of marriage, quite unlike her sister's, involves a deep-rooted antipathy toward men.

When the conversation turns to childbearing, each sister

again reveals her fundamental nature. Ursula, tentative, wary, yet open to the possibility of transcending her present state, observes, with "a dazzled, baffled look," that "one feels [having children] is still beyond one" (p. 3). Gudrun, on the other hand, seems to find the very thought of maternity too disturbing to contemplate. Denying any emotional involvement in the matter, she again withdraws into a self-protective shell, responding to her sister's groping comments with a "mask-like, expressionless face." The emotion that she refuses to acknowledge manifests itself in an irrational animosity toward Ursula and leads her to end the conversation.

The first four pages of *Women in Love* are devoted largely to dialogue, interspersed with brief descriptions of the speaker's tone, facial expression, and gesture. But at two points Lawrence supplements his camera-eye presentation with additional information about his characters. The first such passage focuses largely on Gudrun: "Gudrun was very beautiful, passive, soft-skinned, soft-limbed. She wore a dress of dark-blue silky stuff, with ruches of blue and green linen lace in the neck and sleeves; and she had emerald-green stockings. Her look of confidence and diffidence contrasted with Ursula's sensitive expectancy. The provincial people, intimidated by Gudrun's perfect sang-froid and exclusive bareness of manner, said of her: 'She is a smart woman.' She had just come back from London, where she had spent several years, working at an art-school, as a student, and living a studio life" (p. 2). Lawrence presents Gudrun largely in terms of her physical appearance and outward manner.[33] In describing the impression she makes on others he goes so far as to quote an opinion apparently shared by all "the provincial people." Here, clearly, is a woman who takes considerable pains to transmit a "personality" to her "audience." While Ursula's "sensitive expectancy" suggests a responsiveness to the world around her, Gudrun, revealing a paradoxical combination of assurance and insecurity, seems totally self-absorbed. The statement that she looks at once confident and diffident suggests a deeply divided psyche, as does the "strange grimace, half sly smiling, half anguish" attributed to her a paragraph later.

Lawrence's discussion of Ursula is far more abstract, relying primarily on metaphor rather than direct description: "Ursula having always that strange brightness of an essential flame that is caught, meshed, contravened. She lived a good deal by herself, to herself, working, passing on from day to day, and always thinking, trying to lay hold on life, to grasp it in her own understanding. Her active living was suspended, but underneath, in the darkness, something was coming to pass. If only she could break through the last integuments! She seemed to try and put her hands out, like an infant in the womb, and she could not, not yet. Still she had a strange prescience, an intimation of something yet to come" (p. 3). Lawrence begins his discussion of Ursula with the flame image that he uses in an essay quoted above to represent the ever-changing self. Suggesting that Ursula is entrapped by her surroundings, Lawrence describes her as "caught, meshed, contravened." Telling us nothing about the impression that she makes on other people, Lawrence emphasizes her desire to understand herself and her eagerness for personal growth. Images of gestation and germination indicate that her present identity is far less important than her potential for some kind of rebirth.

A few pages later, as the Brangwen sisters walk through Beldover on their way to a wedding, Lawrence presents another aspect of Gudrun's character: her strange ambivalence toward the ugly mining community to which she has recently returned. Gudrun's speculation upon the motive for her return suggests an attempt to rationalize an unconscious attraction to a world she consciously despises: "It was strange that she should have chosen to come back and test the full effect of this shapeless, barren ugliness upon herself" (p. 5). Her disgust at Beldover's sordidness is mingled with fascination: "Ursula, it's marvelous, it's really marvelous—it's really wonderful, another world" (p. 5). The existence of a world like Beldover has the power to shatter Gudrun's fragile sense of her own identity: "If this were human life, if these were human beings, living in a complete world, then what was her own world, outside? . . . she felt as if she were treading in the air, quite unstable, her heart was contracted, as if at any minute she might be precipitated to the ground" (p. 6). Later in the novel we learn that Gudrun is continually tormented by the conviction that others participate in a reality from which she herself is barred.[34]

The two sisters' behavior upon reaching the church provides further evidence of differences between them. Gudrun, aloof and analytical, observes her fellow guests with the same cold reductive vision that we later associate with her art: "Gudrun watched them closely, with objective curiosity. She saw each one as a complete figure, like a character in a book, or a subject in a picture, or a marionette in a theatre, a finished creation . . . She knew them, they were finished, sealed and stamped and finished with, for her" (p. 8). In sharp contrast to Gudrun's unemotional detachment is Ursula's spontaneous involvement in the proceedings: "She could not bear it that the bride should arrive and no groom. The wedding must not be a fiasco, it must not" (p. 12).

The fascination with violence that will prove to be one of Gudrun's dominant features plays a central part in her initial response to Gerald Crich. She is attracted not only to

Gerald's blond, northern beauty, but also to the "sinister stillness in his bearing, the lurking danger of his unsubdued temper" (p. 9). Upon perceiving Gerald's wolflike nature Gudrun is overwhelmed by desire: "A strange transport took possession of her, all her veins were in a paroxysm of violent sensation" (p. 9). In contrast to Gudrun's precipitous reaction to Gerald, Ursula's response to Birkin seems cautious, tentative, and sane: "Ursula was left thinking about Birkin. He piqued her, attracted her, and annoyed her. She wanted to know him more" (p. 15). Lawrence uses a brief discussion of Birkin by Ursula and Gudrun to substantiate his earlier description of each sister. "What I can't stand about him," Gudrun comments, "is his way with other people—his way of treating any little fool as if she were his greatest consideration. One feels so awfully sold, oneself" (p. 15). Although her self-assured tone creates an impression of confidence, Gudrun's statement reveals a diffidence so great that she cannot see a social inferior treated like herself without a painful loss of self-esteem. Ursula makes no attempt to challenge her sister's judgment: "She was always forced to assent to Gudrun's pronouncements, even when she was not in accord altogether" (p. 15). Although we still have no clear idea of what Ursula may become, we now begin to sense the nature of her entrapment.

The continual contrast between two kinds of human beings that is implicit throughout the first chapter of *Women in Love* is the dominant strategy of the novel as a whole. And just as we receive a more vivid impression of Gudrun than we do of Ursula, we also find Gerald, bound, as Gudrun is, to a consistent set of psychological needs, to be a more coherent character than Birkin, who passes through emotional states so varied that it is sometimes hard to discern in them even the "single radically unchanged element" that Lawrence attributes to the self.[35] When we think of Birkin we remember first of all the theories he espouses. Apart from a fervent commitment to his own ideas he seems to possess no identifying personality traits, and the reader's memory of him probably focuses on particular activities—throwing rocks at a reflection of the moon, perhaps, or walking naked and wounded through thick vegetation or wrestling with Gerald.

It is tempting, particularly in light of the suppressed first chapter of the novel, to ascribe to Birkin one basic psychological drive—latent homosexuality—and to account on this basis for both his erratic behavior and his unconventional opinions. But his role within the novel would be severely undermined by the assumption that, like Gerald, he is at the mercy of unconscious emotional needs that are reflected in all that he says and does. (Far from worrying whether his own views on marriage might be psychologically determined, Birkin fears that they may be merely intellectual constructs with no source in his deepest self. After trying to convince Ursula to accept the kind of relationship he desires, he wonders, "Was it really only an idea, or was it the interpretation of a profound yearning?" [p. 245].)

The absence of consistent personality traits is central to Lawrence's conception of Birkin, whose most fundamental characteristic is an "odd mobility and changeableness which seemed to contain the quintessence of faith" (p. 225). Gerald can be recognized as an inadequate human being precisely because he possesses the restrictive consistency that Birkin lacks. Looking at Gerald, Birkin sees "the man himself, complete, and as if fated, doomed, limited. This strange sense of fatality in Gerald, as if he were limited to one form of existence, one knowledge, one activity, a sort of fatal halfness, which to himself seemed wholeness, always overcame

Birkin after their moments of passionate approach, and filled him with a sort of contempt, or boredom'' (p. 199).[36]

The diametrically opposite modes of being embodied by Gerald and Birkin can best be understood in terms of a theory propounded in ''The Reality of Peace,'' an essay written about the same time as *Women in Love*: ''There are two ways and two goals, as it has always been. And so it will always be. Some are set upon one road, the road of death and undoing, and some are set upon the other road, the road of creation. And the fulfillment of every man is the following his own separate road to its end . . . Every man has his goal, and this there is no altering. Except by asserting the free will. A man may choose nullity. He may choose to absolve himself from his fate either of life or death. He may oppose his self-will, his free will, between life and his own small entity, or between true death and himself.''[37]

While Birkin is intrinsically on the ''road of creation,'' Gerald's natural goal is ''death and undoing.'' His destructiveness first manifests itself during his childhood when he fires a supposedly empty gun at his brother's head. The gun proves to be loaded, and the brother is killed. Through the observations of both Birkin and Ursula, Lawrence makes it clear that this fratricide was no mere accident: without an unconscious wish to kill, one cannot pull the trigger of the ''emptiest gun in the world'' while someone is looking down the barrel. Lawrence also suggests early in the novel that Gerald unconsciously wishes to be killed. When Gerald maintains that the abandonment of social restraints would lead to universal carnage, Birkin declares, ''You seem to have a lurking desire to have your gizzard slit, and imagine every man has his knife up his sleeve for you'' (pp. 27-28).[38]

Refusing to submit to his deepest desires, Gerald fervently

tries to "absolve himself from his fate." His obsession with power is a manifestation of his effort to escape his destined road by sheer force of will. Gerald's work has meaning for him only insofar as it involves the triumph of personal volition over the recalcitrance of external reality: "It was his will to subjugate Matter to his own ends. The subjugation itself was the point, the fight was the be-all, the fruits of victory were mere results . . . What he wanted was the pure fulfillment of his own will in the struggle with the natural conditions" (p. 216). Incapable of a vital existence and yet unwilling to die, Gerald can only "choose nullity," defining his life in purely instrumental terms: "Everything in the world has its function, and is good or not good in so far as it fulfills this function more or less perfectly. Was a miner a good miner? Then he was complete. Was a manager a good manager? That was enough. Gerald himself, who was responsible for all this industry, was he a good director? If he were, he had fulfilled his life" (p. 215).

While Gerald's past exploits as a soldier, explorer, and sportsman seem likely to have involved an unconscious pursuit of death,[39] only once in *Women in Love* does he openly manifest the self-destructiveness that lies hidden beneath his aggressive virility. When his sister falls from a boat and drowns, Gerald drives himself to exhaustion in a futile effort to save her, becoming furious when Birkin opposes his compulsion to continue diving. A short while later he virtually acknowledges his suppressed desire for death: " 'If you once die,' he said, 'then when it's over, it's finished. Why come to life again? There's room under that water there for thousands' " (pp. 175-176).

To escape recognition of his unconscious desires, Gerald formulates a self-image antithetical to his deepest nature. Our early impression of his relationship with Gudrun leads us to expect masochistic submission on her part, sadistic domination on his. This expectation, created by Gudrun's initial response to Gerald in the wedding scene discussed above, is strengthened both when Gudrun watches in rapt fascination while Gerald brutally beats his mare and when Gerald speaks of the "domestication" of women as a kind of sport. But their relationship actually involves submissiveness on his part, domination on hers. The establishment of the first bond between them is described as follows: "Henceforward, she knew, she had her power over him. Wherever they met, they would be secretly associated. And he would be helpless in the association with her" (p. 114). It is immediately after Gudrun predicts that she will "strike the last blow" that Gerald declares his love to her. A short while later, suffering from a hand injury, Gerald allows Gudrun to row him home. This scene provides a paradigm of their relationship: "By her tone he could tell she wanted to have him in the boat to herself, and that she was subtly gratified that she should have power over them both. He gave himself, in a strange, electric submission" (p. 168).

During the final stage of Gerald's relationship with Gudrun it becomes clear that his desire for her is really a longing for death. "There's something final about this," he tells Birkin, "and Gudrun seems like the end to me. I don't know—but she seems so soft, her skin like silk, her arms heavy and soft. And it withers my consciousness, somehow, it burns the pith of my mind" (p. 430). Gerald knows he can save himself from destruction only by willing his independence from Gudrun, but his conscious volition cannot withstand the force of his desire:

He knew that it only needed one convulsion of his will for him to be able to turn upon himself also, to close upon himself as a stone fixes upon itself, and is impervious, self-completed, a thing isolated.

This knowledge threw him into a terrible chaos. Because, however much he might mentally *will* to be immune and self-complete, the desire for this state was lacking, and he could not create it. He could see that, to exist at all, he must be perfectly free of Gudrun, leave her if she wanted to be left, demand nothing of her, have no claim upon her.

But then, to have no claim upon her, he must stand by himself, in sheer nothingness. And his brain turned to nought at the idea. It was a state of nothingness. (P. 436)

From Lawrence's point of view Gerald takes the only road he can legitimately pursue. In the terms that Lawrence uses in "The Reality of Peace," Gerald can save himself from death only so long as he chooses "nullity," opposing his free will "between true death and himself." "Why should he close up and become impervious, immune, like a partial thing in a sheath," Gerald asks himself, "when he had broken forth, like a seed that has germinated, to issue forth in being, embracing the unrealised heavens" (p. 437). The metaphor with which Lawrence describes Gerald's state at this point in the novel is precisely the one he uses to represent Ursula's condition in the optimistic conclusion of *The Rainbow,* where he writes, "And again, to her feverish brain, came the vivid reality of acorns in February lying on the floor of a wood with their shells burst and discarded and the kernel issued naked to put itself forth. She was the naked, clear kernel thrusting forth the clear, powerful shoot."[40] Ursula, intrinsically on the road to life, escapes from the shell of her former existence to become a vital individual. Gerald, set on the road to death, can escape from the sheath of his will only by acquiescing in his destruction.

When Gerald is asked early in the novel whether he has ever been afraid, he replies, "Yes, I'm afraid of some things—of being shut up, locked up anywhere—or being fastened. I'm afraid of being bound hand and foot" (p. 59). Once again Lawrence uses Gerald's conscious fear as an index of his unconscious desire. While his volitional self dreads nothing more than the enforced passivity imposed by physical constraint, his deepest self longs to rest within a womblike enclosure. The state he achieves through the sexual act approximates prenatal life: "Mother and substance of all life she was. And he, child and man, received of her and was made whole . . . the miraculous, soft effluence of her breast suffused over him, over his seared, damaged brain, like a healing lymph, like a soft, soothing flow of life itself, perfect as if he were bathed in the womb again" (p. 337). Lawrence's suggestive description of the snow-covered mountains where Gerald ultimately dies instructs us to regard his death as another return to the womb: "at the end, like the navel of the earth, a white-folded wall, and two peaks glimmering in the late light. Straight in front ran the cradle of silent snow, between the great slopes that were fringed with a little roughness of pine trees, like hair, round the base" (pp. 390-391).[41] Gerald immediately senses in this landscape the entrapment that he both dreads and desires: "He saw the blind valley, the great cul-de-sac of snow and mountain peaks under the heaven. And there was no way out" (p. 391).

Gerald's final moment of consciousness corroborates Lawrence's earlier suggestion that his fear of being murdered is a longing in disguise. Even as he succumbs to his profound desire for death, Gerald persists in denying his own self-destructiveness by seeing himself as the victim of an external assailant: "He was bound to be murdered, he could see it.

This was the moment when the death was uplifted, and there was no escape . . . He could feel the blow descending, he knew he was murdered'' (p. 465).

There is undoubtedly a great deal to argue with in the assumptions that underlie Lawrence's portrayal of Gerald as intrinsically bound for death. But however objectionable his theoretical framework may be, Lawrence's depiction of this character reflects a profound insight into psychopathology, anticipating with stiking precision subsequent clinical findings. Many years after the publication of *Women in Love* Karl Menninger concluded that the act of suicide requires three independent conditions: the wish to kill, the wish to be killed, and the wish to die.[42] In his tendency toward violence, his preoccupation with being murdered, and his profound longing for passivity, Gerald clearly manifests each of these separate desires. Interestingly, Menninger cites as typical signs of an unconscious wish to kill the very traits that Lawrence attributes to Gerald: the childhood desire to destroy a sibling and the capacity to derive sensual pleasure from beating a horse. Menninger further maintains that suicidal tendencies most frequently occur in individuals whose personal relationships are strongly ambivalent and that these tendencies are fostered by a situation that "makes it suddenly necessary to reinvest love and particularly hate through the sudden interruption or threatened interruption" of an established relationship (p. 29). Gerald's feelings toward Gudrun are, of course, exceedingly ambivalent, and Gudrun's rejection of Gerald in favor of Loerke constitutes exactly the kind of interruption Menninger describes. Finally, Menninger observes that suicide is most commonly attempted when the wish to kill, unexpectedly deprived of an external object, is turned back upon the self. Once again *Women in Love* anticipates Menninger's findings, for it is immediately after his vain attempt to take Gudrun's life that Gerald puts an end to his own.

In the previous chapter we observed an unresolved tension in *The Red and the Black* between a Romantic approach to personal identity and suggestions of unconscious motivation. The psychological coherence of Stendhal's portrait of Julien tends to conflict with our perception of him as a Romantic hero. Lawrence avoids such ambiguity in *Women in Love* by his use of two contrasting protagonists. While his portrayal of Birkin embodies a Romantic conception of the vital, spontaneous self, his depiction of Gerald suggests that psychological reality is often very far from this ideal.

By attributing the longing to be "absorbed" by a woman to the death-seeking Gerald, Lawrence seems to dissociate himself from any such desire. But Lawrence's most personal writings suggest that this aspect of Gerald's character is by no means wholly alien to his creator. Paul Morel, the protagonist of Lawrence's autobiographical novel *Sons and Lovers*, feels surprisingly little ambivalence toward his mother's domination. But his relationship with his girlfriend Miriam reflects a complex response to the idea of being possessed by a woman. He finds in Miriam a proprietary quality similar to his mother's that attracts him in spite of his resentment: "She did not want to meet him so that there were two of them, man and woman together. She wanted to draw all of him into her. It urged him to an intensity like madness which fascinated him, as drug-taking might."[43] Paul's intense ambivalence toward dependence on a woman remains unexplored and unresolved; in the final pages of the novel Miriam is accused both of being too possessive ("You love me so much, you want to put me in your pocket. And I should die there smothered"; p. 417) and of not being possessive enough ("It was the end then between them. She could not take him and relieve him of the responsibility of himself"; p. 418).

Lawrence's own capacity for a painful degree of dependence upon a sexual partner is most openly revealed in the parts of *Look! We Have Come Through!* that describe his early relationship with Frieda. Such poems as "Quite Forsaken," "Forsaken and Forlorn," "Song of a Man Who Is Not Loved," "Mutilation," and "Humiliation" convey Lawrence's unhappiness during Frieda's temporary absences, his agonizing fear of losing her, and his frustration at his own dependency. In a poem entitled "Wedlock" Lawrence explicitly demands of his wife a love that is maternal as well as conjugal: "Nourish me, and endue me, I am only of you, / I am your issue."[44] The intensity of his need for his partner understandably leads to ambivalence, and Lawrence declares in "Both Sides of the Medal" that since passion invariably imprisons one human being in the "orbit" of another, hatred is an unavoidable result of love. But in "Manifesto," one of the final poems in this volume, Lawrence at last envisions an escape from the pain of overdependence. Criticizing Frieda for her failure to acknowledge him as something apart from herself, Lawrence postulates an ideal conjunction of two "pure, isolated, complete" beings that closely resembles the star-equilibrium described in *Women in Love*. Thus, unlike Rousseau, who frankly accepts his desire to combine the status of lover with that of son, Lawrence repudiates with great vehemence any attraction he may feel to a filial role.

IN *Women in Love* Gerald's desire to be absorbed by a woman is viewed as a pathological symptom. When Birkin lapses from psychological health, he takes the opposite direction from excessive dependency, recoiling from all emotional involvement. Lying "sick and unmoved, in pure opposition to everything," he sees sex as a threat to his integrity: "On the whole, he hated sex, it was such a limitation. It was sex that turned a man into a broken half of a couple, the woman into the other broken half. And he wanted to be single in himself, the woman single in herself. He wanted sex to revert to the level of the other appetites, to be regarded as a functional process, not as a fulfillment" (p. 191). Birkin longs to replace the "merging, the clutching, the mingling of love" with a new kind of conjunction, "where man had being and woman had being, two pure beings, each constituting the freedom of the other, balancing each other like two poles of one force, like two angels, or two demons" (p. 191). There is, however, reason to suspect that such a union might be more satisfying to the man Birkin would like to be than to the man he in fact is: "He wanted so much to be free, not under the compulsion of any need for unification" (p. 191). But a short while later, taking no account of his own unwelcome need for "unification," Birkin attributes his dread of sex solely to the possessiveness that he regards as a universal female trait: "But it seemed to him, woman was always so horrible and clutching, she had such a lust for possession, a greed of self-importance in love. She wanted to have, to own, to control, to be dominant. Everything must be referred back to her, to Woman, the Great Mother of everything, out of whom proceeded everything and to whom everything must finally be rendered up" (p. 192).

While Birkin regards the traditional conception of love as an instrument of female possessiveness, Ursula suspects that the alternative he proposes, "an equilibrium, a pure balance of two single beings:—as the stars balance each other" (p. 139), may be simply a rationale for masculine domination. Not wholly enthusiastic about Birkin's idea of marriage when it is explained to her in abstract terms, Ursula becomes considerably less so a moment later when, watching a male cat cuff a female into submission, Birkin uses this example of feline machismo to exemplify his theory. Birkin's approval of the bullying Mino would seem to justify Ursula's insistence that the relationship he wants resembles not two balanced stars but a planet and its satellite. There appears, however, to be a strong element of self-parody in Birkin's defense of Mino's attempt "to bring this female cat into a pure stable equilibrium, a transcendent and abiding rapport with the single male" (p. 142). And when Ursula vigorously accuses him of having given himself away, Birkin responds with "frustration and amusement and irritation and admiration and love" (p. 142). It is hard to know what to make of this seeming defense of male domination in which a woman has the last word. Not yet committed to the doctrine of female subordination that informs his subsequent novels, Lawrence seems to imply in this scene that a man's conviction that masculine dominance is ordained by natural law is on shaky ground indeed if the woman he loves does not find it natural to submit.[45]

Birkin hesitates to marry Ursula because he suspects in her a determination to possess him by means of a self-abnegating, quasi-maternal love: "She was only too ready to knock her head on the ground before a man. But this was only when she was so certain of her man, that she could worship him as a woman worships her own infant, with a worship of perfect possession" (p. 192). But in Lawrence's actual portrayal of Ursula, a worshipful devotion to Birkin is less in evidence than a tendency toward what might appear to be an exaggerated version of Birkin's own ideal—a "singleness" so pure that it precludes any form of communion. For a period of time Ursula feels herself wholly self-contained: "One was a tiny little rock with the tide of nothingness rising higher and higher. She herself was real, and only herself—just like a rock in a wash of flood-water. The rest was all nothingness. She was hard and indifferent, isolated in herself" (pp. 236-237). The maternal possessiveness that Birkin fears in Ursula and the self-isolating coldness that she displays through much of the chapter entitled "Moony" probably strike most readers as very different qualities. For Lawrence, however, they seem to constitute two manifestations of a single reality.[46] This is made particularly evident in the pages immediately following Birkin's proposal of marriage, which Ursula irrationally interprets as an attempt to "bully" her. Her independence now reaches its peak: "Recoiling upon herself, she became hard and self-completed, like a jewel. She was bright and invulnerable, quite free and happy, perfectly liberated in her self-possession . . . She would go on now for days like this, in this bright frank state of seemingly pure spontaneity, so essentially oblivious of the existence of anything but herself" (p. 254). Yet it is precisely while she is in this state that we see Ursula at her most maternal: "Ursula saw her men as sons, pitied their yearning and admired their courage, and wondered over them as a mother wonders over her child" (p. 255).[47]

The language used to describe Ursula's self-sufficient state ("hard and self-completed," "stable in resistance," "perfectly liberated in her self-possession") is generally associated in Lawrence's writing with the conscious ego. Thus despite Ursula's "seemingly pure spontaneity" her isolation is presumably a product of sheer volition rather than natural impulse. Hovering at the brink of a permanent commitment that she desires yet hesitates to make, she, like Gerald, sheathes herself in her will out of fear of her genuine instincts. But she, of course, finally sloughs off her sheath to embrace not death, but love.

When she emerges from egoistic isolation, Ursula immediately longs for an opposite mode of existence—a complete abnegation of the self before the concept of love and before the beloved partner. But Lawrence suggests that Ursula is no less possessive when she contemplates total surrender to Birkin than when she condescendingly regards him as her child: "She believed that love was *everything*. Man must render himself up to her. He must be quaffed to the dregs by her. Let him be *her man* utterly, and she in return would be his humble slave—whether she wanted it or not" (p. 258).

Rejecting both self-willed isolation and surrender of the self to another, Birkin longs for a union that will not violate the individuality of each partner: "There was the paradisal entry into pure, single being, the individual soul taking precedence over love and desire for union, stronger than any pangs of emotion, a lovely state of free proud singleness, which accepted the obligation of the permanent connection with others, and with the other, submits to the yoke and leash of love, but never forfeits its own proud individual singleness, even while it loves and yields" (p. 247). While Ursula can conceive of abandoning herself only to a force that transcends the individual, Birkin espouses self-abandon of a very different kind: the surrender of one's conscious will to one's own deepest being. Early in the novel he declares: "You've got to lapse out before you can know what sensual reality is, lapse into unknowingness, and give up your volition. You've got to do it. You've got to learn no[t]-to-be, before you can come into being" (p. 37). In propounding his theory of love to Ursula he explains: "I deliver *myself* over to the unknown, in coming to you, I am without reserves or defences, stripped entirely, into the unknown. Only there needs the pledge between us, that we will both cast off everything, cast off ourselves even, and cease to be, so that that which is perfectly ourselves can take place in us'' (p. 138). Although Ursula is willing to give herself up completely to Birkin, she is not quite satisfactory as a lover, even in the last section of the novel, because she cannot wholly submit to her own impulses: "She gave herself up in delight to being loved by him. She knew that, in spite of his joy when she abandoned herself, he was a little bit saddened too. She could give herself up to his activity. But she could not be herself, she *dared* not come forth quite nakedly to his nakedness, abandoning all adjustment, lapsing in pure faith with him'' (p. 426).

Lawrence continually struggles to describe subjective experiences for which no vocabulary exists. The problems intrinsic to this endeavor become particularly acute when he sets out to distinguish the kind of self-abandon that he advocates from other emotional experiences that this term might suggest. Since it is extremely difficult either to explain or to dramatize the precise psychological state that he values so highly, Lawrence relies heavily on contrasts to elucidate his meaning. The ego abandonment that Birkin insists on is not the giving of oneself to another that Ursula is able to achieve, the mind-obliterating physical sensation represented by the African statue, or the Dionysic impulse "to let go, to fling away everything, and lapse into a sheer unrestraint, brutal and licentious'' that Gerald and Gudrun share (p. 279). It is not an abdication of individuality, but a fulfillment of one's own deepest nature; not a frenzied passion, but a state of calm content. "I hate ecstasy,'' Birkin declares, "Dionysic or any other. It's like going round in a squirrel cage. I want you not to care about yourself, just to be there and not to care about yourself, not to insist—be glad and sure and indifferent'' (p. 243). A short while later Lawrence attempts to describe the experience of nonbeing that enables one to become what one truly is: ''She clung nearer to him. He held her close, and kissed her softly, gently. It was such peace and heavenly freedom, just to fold her and kiss her gently, and not to have any thoughts or any desires or any will, just to be still with her, to be perfectly still and together, in a peace that was not sleep, but content in bliss'' (p. 244).

Whether Lawrence is writing about the self or the couple, his theories reflect the same conflict between two opposing desires: preservation of a sense of discrete individuality and transcendence of the self-conscious ego. By defining individuality as something wholly independent of consciousness, Lawrence convinces himself that it is possible to escape from the ego without loss of personal integrity. The sexual doctrine propounded in *Women in Love* further reconciles his conflicting emotional needs. Both man and woman must maintain their singleness, he insists, submitting not to each other but to their own deepest selves. By conceptualizing the sexual act in this way, Lawrence simultaneously justifies the ego transcendence that he desires and wards off the female possessiveness that he fears.

Lawrence is not completely consistent, however, in his description of the ideal sexual union. It is difficult to reconcile Birkin's insistence that his relationship with Ursula must be a balance between two single, separate beings who never merge into one with the following passage:

> In the new, superfine bliss, a peace superseding knowledge, there was no I and you, there was only the third, unrealized wonder, the wonder of existing not as oneself, but in a consummation of my being and of her being in a new one, a new,

paradisal unit regained from the duality. How can I say "I love you" when I have ceased to be, and you have ceased to be: we are both caught up and transcended into a new oneness where everything is silent, because there is nothing to answer, all is perfect and at one. Speech travels between the separate parts. But in the perfect One there is perfect silence of bliss. (Pp. 361-362)

This rhapsodic celebration of perfect oneness suggests a longing on Lawrence's part incompatible with the "pure, single being" that he so highly values. But his association of conjugal love with female possessiveness and male dependency prevents him from endorsing such oneness with a woman as a valid ideal.[48] Thus despite the apparent success of his relationship with Ursula, Birkin concludes that he cannot be truly happy without a second relationship with a man, a relationship that would provide a less threatening kind of union and at the same time preserve him from Ursula's efforts to "quaff him to the dregs."[49]

THE idea that men, unlike women, require a means of self-fulfillment outside the sexual bond is a recurrent theme in Lawrence's works. His expository writings repeatedly suggest that this masculine need can best be fulfilled through communal participation and productive labor. As early as the "Study of Thomas Hardy" he identifies "Public Good" and "Community" with the male principle, "Self-Establishment" with the female. "The male exists in doing," he declares, "the female in being" (p. 481). His association of purposive activity with masculinity is so strong that he regards a commitment to work as the identifying characteristic of genuine manhood. A "true male," he declares, will "see his job through, at no matter what cost. A man is strictly only himself when he is fulfilling some purpose he has conceived"

(p. 483).[50] Lawrence has considerable difficulty, however, in reconciling his belief in a masculine need for purposive activity with his perception of the brutalizing nature of work in the modern world.[51]

By the time Lawrence wrote *Women in Love,* a number of circumstances, including the suppression of *The Rainbow,* the First World War, and his own treatment as a suspected spy, made him deeply pessimistic about contemporary society. In the original first chapter of the novel he suggested that the climate of the times precluded worthwhile communal endeavor: "Birkin was just coming to a knowledge of the essential futility of all attempt at social unanimity in constructiveness. In the winter, there can only be unanimity of disintegration."[52] In the world portrayed in *Women in Love* man's natural desire to "fulfill some purpose he has conceived" can find no outlet except the sterile mechanical activity epitomized by Gerald Crich and the miners he employs. Temporarily repudiating his belief that "the male exists in doing," Lawrence focuses his attention in this novel on the individual's search for self-fulfillment in a world that provides no basis for meaningful action.

Like most nineteenth-century Romantic heroes, Rupert Birkin is an outsider both by nature and by choice. Early in the novel we learn that he is constitutionally unfit for communal participation: "His nature was clever and separate, he did not fit at all in the conventional occasion. Yet he subordinated himself to the common idea, travestied himself" (p. 14). One of the rare characters in the history of the English novel to deliberately refuse to be part of his society, Birkin symbolically repudiates communal membership by the act of resigning his job as school inspector: "If I find I can live sufficiently by myself . . . I shall give up my work altogether. It has become dead to me. I don't believe in the humanity I pretend to be part of, I don't care a straw for the social ideals I live by, I hate the dying organic form of social mankind—so it can't be anything but trumpery, to work at education. I shall drop it as soon as I am clear enough—to-morrow perhaps—and be by myself'' (p. 124).[53]

Women in Love, like *The Red and The Black*, is among other things a novel about the plight of the individual who finds himself in a society that he can neither accept nor change. Stendhal's protagonist, unable to envision a means of self-realization outside the established social world, strives for success within this world despite his contempt for its values. In *Women in Love*, however, the only characters who care about status and achievement are those who share the pervasive corruption of their society: those who can see the contemporary world for what it is must seek an extrasocial basis for their existence. Near the beginning of the novel Lawrence suggests that in the absence of both religious and social faith, a perfect relationship with a woman is the only value that can still give meaning to life: "It seems to me there remains only this perfect union with a woman—sort of ultimate marriage," Birkin declares, "and there isn't anything else" (p. 51). By the end of the novel, still convinced that personal relationships are the only goals worth pursuing, Birkin believes that he would have been completely happy if he could only have had a second "perfect" union with Gerald to supplement the one he has attained.

Since Gerald Crich embodies so much that Lawrence despises, it is tempting to conclude, as David Gordon has done, that Lawrence erred in employing a single character both as a representative of the world of power and position and as "the irreplaceable member of a necessary new society."[54] But however awkward it may be on the literal level of the text, this dual use of Gerald is in fact essential to the novel's meaning.

Despite his success in depicting Gerald as a highly convincing individual, Lawrence intends his portrait of this "industrial magnate" not merely as a case history of a self-destructive man, but as a prototype of the almost ubiquitous morbidity of a world on the road to death. Thus virtually any man Birkin might have chosen to be his eternal friend would presumably have shared Gerald's destructive nature. Of all the characters who appear in this novel, none but Birkin and Ursula have a genuine instinct for life. Because the world in which he finds himself precludes vital masculine communion as well as creative endeavor, Birkin is left with only his doctrine of singleness to save him from "absorption" by his wife.

At the end of *Women in Love* Birkin suggests that his marriage can make his life at least bearable if not completely happy. "Having you," he tells Ursula, "I can live all my life without anybody else, any other sheer intimacy" (p. 472). But Lawrence soon becomes far more pessimistic about the kind of existence that Birkin has no choice but to accept. In *Fantasia of the Unconscious* Lawrence declares, "When man loses his deep sense of purposive, creative activity, he feels lost, and is lost. When he makes the sexual consummation the supreme consummation, even in his *secret* soul, he falls into the beginnings of despair. When he makes woman, or the woman and child the great centre of life and of life-significance, he falls into the beginnings of despair" (p. 143).

IN Lawrence's writings through *Women in Love* we find repeated suggestions that women, desiring to possess the men they love, constitute a threat to masculine independence. In the works that immediately follow this novel Lawrence strives to reduce the significance of the sexual bond, thereby minimizing woman's power over her mate. In *Fantasia of the Unconscious* he explicitly relegates woman to a secondary role in her partner's life. One of his arguments rests on man's need to surpass woman through his solitary achievements: "Primarily and supremely man is *always* the pioneer of life, adventuring onward into the unknown, *alone with his own temerarious, dauntless soul.* Woman for him exists only in the twilight, by the camp fire, when day has departed" (pp. 143-144; second italics mine). However, Lawrence completely reverses the basis of his argument only a paragraph later, this time proposing communal rather than individual achievement as man's primary goal: "We have to break away, back to the great unison of manhood in some passionate *purpose.* Now this is not like sex. Sex is always individual . . . We have got to get back to the great purpose of manhood, a passionate unison in actively making a world. This is a real commingling of many. And in such a commingling we forfeit the individual" (p. 144). The juxtaposition of these two contradictory passages suggests that Lawrence's deepest concern at this time is neither individuality nor communion, but rather any purely masculine goal that can free the male from dependence upon a woman.

In the two novels that follow *Women in Love*, as in *Fantasia of the Unconscious*, Lawrence shifts his focus away from heterosexual love, exploring possibilities for eliminating or counterbalancing the bond between a man and a woman. But these works reflect even more clearly than *Women in Love* the paradoxical Romantic desire to raise the individual self to the status of an absolute and also to transcend the isolated ego by merging with a larger whole.

One of the most striking features of both *Aaron's Rod* and *Kangaroo* is the repeated assertion of two antithetical ideas: the absolute singleness and self-responsibility of every individual and the desirability of a social communion based on the submission of the weak to the strong. Rawdon Lilly, the character in *Aaron's Rod* who most closely resembles his creator, openly acknowledges the incompatibility of these two propositions. In a scene that has become infamous for its fascistic overtones, Lilly argues vehemently for "a real committal of the life-issue of inferior beings to the responsibility of a superior being."[55] A moment later, however, he declares, "But I should say the blank opposite with just as much fervour . . . I think every man is a sacred and holy individual, *never* to be violated. I think there is only one thing I hate to the verge of madness, and that is *bullying*" (p. 273).[56] Lilly is by no means simply playing devil's advocate in espousing these mutually exclusive positions, for the earnest dialogue with which the novel concludes reaffirms his commitment to both. In trying to convince Aaron to repudiate his "love urge," Lilly insists on the necessity of taking full responsibility for oneself:

> You can't lose yourself, so stop trying. The responsibility is on your own shoulders all the time, and no God which man has ever struck can take it off. You *are* yourself and so *be* yourself. Stick to it and abide by it. Passion or no passion, ecstasy or no ecstasy, urge or no urge, there's no goal outside you, where you can consummate like an eagle flying into the sun, or a moth into a candle . . . You've got an innermost, integral unique self, and since it's the only thing you have got or ever will have, don't go trying to lose it. (Pp. 285-286)

But four pages later he reverses his argument completely, insisting that Aaron's only hope for survival is to submit himself to the power of a greater man: "You, Aaron, you too have the need to submit. You, too, have the need livingly to yield to a more heroic soul, to give yourself. You know you

have. And you know it isn't love. It is life-submission. And
you know it. But you kick against the pricks. And perhaps
you'd rather die than yield. And so, die you must'' (pp. 289-
290).

Kangaroo reflects the same irreconcilable conflict between
individualistic and hierarchical values. Richard Lovat Somers,
the Lawrence-like protagonist of this novel, asserts with
obsessive frequency the all-importance of the isolate, absolute self. But his ideal of complete self-sufficiency coexists
with a belief in a human need for an authoritarian order:
''One cannot live a life of entire loneliness, like a monkey on
a stick . . . There's got to be meeting: even communion.
Well, then, let us have the other communion . . . Sacrifice to
the strong, not to the weak. In awe, not in dribbling love.
The communion in power.''[57]

In *Aaron's Rod* Lawrence suggests that men may have to
repudiate women entirely in order to achieve genuine self-
fulfillment. The protagonist of *Kangaroo*, however, believes
marriage can be a satisfactory arrangement provided the wife
agrees to be subordinate to her husband: ''She was to submit
to the mystic man and male in him, with reverence, and even
a little awe . . . You can't have two masters of one ship:
neither can you have a ship without a master'' (p. 176). But
as long as Somers, like Birkin at the end of *Women in Love*, is
deprived of any purely male communion, he remains far too
dependent upon his wife to succeed in becoming her master:
''He was the most forlorn and isolated creature in the world,
without even a dog to his command. He was so isolated he
was hardly a man at all, among men. He had absolutely
nothing but her'' (p. 177). Somers's involvement in
Australian politics appears to be motivated largely by a need
for a purely male activity from which his wife can be excluded:

For two or three years now, since the war, he had talked like this about doing some work with men alone, sharing some activity with men . . . It would be out of [Harriet's] sphere, outside the personal sphere of their two lives, and he would keep it there. She emphatically opposed this principle of her externality. She agreed with the necessity for impersonal activity, but oh, she insisted on being identified with the activity, impersonal or not. And he insisted that it could not and should not be: that the pure male activity should be womanless, beyond woman." (Pp. 93-94).[58]

Ultimately repudiating both the socialistic laborites who advocate rule by the masses and the fascistic "Diggers" who espouse social unity through love, Somers tellingly groups "love," "the masses," "the weak," and "woman" together among the forces whose ascendancy must be ended by a countervailing power: "When the flow is sympathetic, or love, then the weak, the woman, the masses, assume the positivity. But the balance even is only kept by stern *authority* [*sic*], the unflinching obstinacy of the return-force, of power" (p. 309). Somers has sought a pure male activity that would place him beyond woman only to find the male world of politics under the sway of essentially "feminine" forces. Nowhere in the contemporary world can he find the power-based communion that alone seems to offer freedom from the threat of domination through love.

The Plumed Serpent is a very different book from the other two "leadership novels" with which it is frequently grouped. The protagonists of both *Aaron's Rod* and *Kangaroo* are essentially powerless men, and their commitment to both individual singleness and masculine communion seems closely related to their fear of female domination. But the male protagonists of *The Plumed Serpent* have a power within them that assures them of ascendancy over women. When contemplating a world where female subservience is the norm, Lawrence seems to lose his concern for individual singleness. In direct contradiction to a view expounded in *Women in Love*,[59] Lawrence, speaking through Kate, attacks the very concept of individual wholeness: "There was no such animal [as an individual]. Except in the mechanical world. In the world of machines, the individual machine is effectual. The individual, like the perfect being, does not and cannot exist, in the vivid world. We are all fragments. And at the best, halves" (p. 426).[60]

In *Kangaroo* Somers predicts that his wife will submit to him only when he himself submits to the power of his unconscious: "Before Harriet would ever accept him, Richard Lovat, as a Lord and Master, he, this selfsame Richard who was so strong on kingship, must open the doors of his soul and let in a dark Lord and Master for himself, the dark god he had sensed outside the door. Let him once truly submit to the dark majesty, break open his doors to this fearful god who is master, and enters us from below, the lower doors; let himself once admit a Master, the unspeakable god: and the rest would happen" (p. 178). But Somers apparently remains incapable of such submission, and his difficulties with Harriet rest unresolved at the end of the book. In *The Plumed Serpent* the metaphorical dark god identified in this passage finds embodiment in the literal gods of a primitive religion. By submitting themselves to the majesty of these deities, Ramón and Cipriano attain a potency that makes them triumphant leaders of a masculine world and revered masters of women.

The sense of a cohesive community that is so central to *The Plumed Serpent* is absent from Lawrence's last two works of fiction, which, like his earlier novels, seem to hold out hope only for those who reject society entirely.[61] In *Apoca-*

lypse, however, Lawrence provides a final affirmation of a communal ideal that can find fulfillment only in a world very different from our own. Repudiating his earlier glorification of the detached nonconformist, he now perceives a universal desire for personal independence as the fundamental illness of our age: "We *cannot bear connection*. That is our malady. We *must* break away, and be isolate. We call that being free, being individual. Beyond a certain point, which we have reached, it is suicide."[62] At the end of a peripatetic, highly individualistic life that prevented him from being truly a part of any family, community, or nation, Lawrence concludes that human happiness requires a sense of organic connection with a world beyond the self: "My individualism is really an illusion. I am a part of the great whole, and I can never escape. But I *can* deny my connections, break them, and become a fragment. Then I am wretched. What we want is to destroy our false, inorganic connections, especially those related to money, and re-establish the living organic connections, with the cosmos, the sun and earth, with mankind and nation and family" (p. 200). Throughout much of his life Lawrence, like Rousseau, combined an exceptionally intense preoccupation with his own individuality and a deep-rooted longing to transcend the isolated ego. Having enraged their countrymen and alienated their friends, both men spent their final days in virtual isolation celebrating an all-encompassing oneness.

3

André Malraux

Radically different from one another in their fundamental values, D. H. Lawrence and André Malraux nevertheless define their subject matter in strikingly similar terms. Closely paralleling Lawrence's assertion that "the business of art is to reveal the relation between man and his circumambient universe," Malraux declares that what interests him most in any man are "certain characteristics which express not so much an individual personality as a particular relationship with the world."[1] Both Lawrence and Malraux reject the traditional assumption that novelists must assign their characters clearly defined personalities,[2] and both regard the conventional domain of the novel—individuals' relationships with each other—as only one part of the complex problem of personal identity. But although Lawrence and Malraux sometimes ask similar questions, their answers reflect diametrically opposite views of the self.

Lawrence believes man's genuine identity includes every facet of his being except the conscious will; Malraux equates the self precisely with this will. Lawrence values consciousness only insofar as it helps an individual fulfill his inherent nature and declares self-knowledge to be not an end but a means. Malraux, on the other hand, attributes great value to consciousness itself, suggesting that a man can make the best of his life by "converting as wide a range of experience as possible into conscious thought." He regards the cultivation of consciousness as an important collective as well as individual goal: "The whole destiny of what men have grouped together under the name of culture, is enclosed in a single idea: to transform destiny into awareness."[3]

Rejecting a dualistic view of man, D. H. Lawrence maintains that an individual's physical and psychological states are intimately related. He not only regards corporal illness as "one of the manifestations of the spirit" but even suggests that an apparently accidental death may have a psychological cause: "Perhaps the soul issues its own ticket of death, when it can stand no more."[4] But to Malraux the involuntary nature of physiological responses identifies the body as an entity apart from the true self. In *The Royal Way* he describes Perken, paralyzed by fear, as "mastered by his flesh, his sinews—by all that can rebel against man."[5] The anticipation of death intensifies one's awareness of the discontinuity between body and mind. Struck with a fatal illness, Perken undergoes with Yeatsian intensity the sensation of being fastened to a dying animal: "He was at once bound to his body and detached from it, like the criminals of old time who were condemned to death by drowning, tied to a corpse. Within him death lay in wait, but so alien, so apart from him" (p. 208).

Lawrence attributes artistic achievement to unconscious impulses that may bear no relation to the artist's conscious concerns.[6] Malraux, valuing art largely as a triumph of the creative will, excludes from this designation any work that does not represent the fulfillment of a volitional intention. He argues, for example, that children's drawings involve a "surrender" to the world and are therefore wholly distinct from mature art, which constitutes "an attempt to take possession of it."[7] Works created by the insane also lack the element of intentionality that Malraux considers central to genuine art. The madman may appear to be a true artist because he "has broken with the outside world. And every break of this sort has the appearance, anyhow, of a conquest." But since the madman's escape from convention is not volitional, it is in fact an imprisonment and not a liberation.[8] Malraux draws an analogy between the art of the madman and that of the savage: both seem to be "an expression of total freedom," yet neither is the product of an individual will.[9] He attributes a contemporary interest in primitive art to the rebirth of a fatalistic view of existence. For primitive fetishes to have become meaningful to civilized man, he declares, it was necessary that "the white races as a whole should abandon that belief in Free Will which since the days of Rome had been the white man's birthright. He had to consent to the supremacy of that part of him which belongs to the dark underworld of being."[10]

When the existence of a "dark underworld of being" has been acknowledged at all, this underworld has generally been perceived as the determining factor in human behavior, an element inherent in man's nature that calls into question the very concept of free choice. The Naturalist and the Freudian both suggest that man's subjective sense of freedom may be only an illusion. Even writers like Conrad and Faulkner, who stop short of accepting a total determinism that would render all moral questions meaningless, believe the dark side of man's nature sometimes supersedes his will. Both Lawrence and Malraux, however, assume that man has the ability to choose whether conscious volition or irrational instinct is to govern his existence. But whereas Lawrence urges man to repudiate his will and submit to unconscious impulse, Malraux exhorts him to make precisely the opposite choice: "First, we proclaim as values not the unconscious but conscience, not abandonment but will."[11]

Although both Lawrence and Malraux acknowledge the existence of hidden forces within the psyche, neither extends a warm welcome to the psychologist who would illuminate the dark side of the mind. Psychology itself is ambiguous in its implications, tending to undercut traditional notions of man's grandeur but also promising to extend the realm of human reason. Depending on whether man is regarded as the knower or the known, a psychological approach to human behavior can either enhance or diminish his stature. Lawrence condemns man's attempts to pry into the psyche as a means of aggrandizing an already too bloated ego. Malraux, on the other hand, believes that in order to bear the humiliations inherent in the human condition the ego needs all the help it can get, including a sense of dignity that psychological probing tends to undermine. He complains, for example, that psychoanalytic studies of artists needlessly expose "the small, pathetic secrets of those few men who did most to make good the honor of being man."[12]

Nowhere is the opposition between Lawrence and Malraux clearer than in their conceptions of physical love. Lawrence, attributing the anguish of modern man to a denial of his true nature, suggests that sexual fulfillment can restore us to spiritual health. Malraux, who regards this anguish as a lucid response to the human condition, believes that sexual love can at best distract us from our pain: "Perhaps love is above all the means which the Occidental uses to free himself from man's fate."[13] Unable to conceive of personal identity apart from the conscious will, Malraux interprets the kind of sexuality advocated by Lawrence as a negation of individuality, a rejection of a unique self in favor of a biological norm. In an essay on *Lady Chatterley's Lover* Malraux writes, "In [Lawrence's] eyes, it is not by the awareness of what he possesses, in particular, that the individual fathoms himself, but rather by the most profound awareness of what he has in common with so many others: his sex . . . he believes it more important, for himself, to be a man than to be an individual."[14] This analysis rests upon a dichotomy that is central to Malraux's thinking but wholly absent from Lawrence's. It would never occur to Lawrence that one might choose between being an individual and being a man, since individuality as he envisions it can be realized only by fulfilling one's sexual nature.

Malraux is disturbed (quite validly, I believe) by the impersonal nature of the relationship between Lady Chatterley and Mellors: "I am suspicious of the guarantees one must look for in the most profound regions of flesh and blood. I consequently fear both their nature and their continuance; for a great flavor of solitude accompanies these creatures of Lawrence. For this preacher of the 'couple,' the 'other' is scarcely to be considered. Conflict or agreement is established between the being and his sensation" (p. 57). But, still equating individuality with the conscious ego, Malraux misinterprets Lawrence's conception of the sexual bond when he concludes that since personalities play no part in a Lawrentian relationship there will be no commitment to a single partner.[15] In fact, while Malraux's sexually active male characters seek continual conquests (one going so far as to possess two women at once), Lawrence's protagonists tend to be monogamous by nature.

Lawrence's fiction repeatedly suggests that the inability to relax one's will during the act of love is an all-too-common failing among women. Malraux, on the other hand, suggests that arousal automatically deprives a woman of the power of conscious volition. Outside the bedroom, Valérie, Ferral's mistress in *Man's Fate*, possesses a determination comparable to that of Lawrence's most self-assertive female characters. But when she is erotically stimulated she becomes helpless before Ferral's will. Malraux's depiction of the female sexual role, which he apparently assumes to be intrinsically passive, reflects the assumption that human dignity rests upon volitional assertion. Ferral can perceive Valérie's pleasure only as a humiliating subjection: "He imagined himself as her, inhabiting her body, feeling in her place that enjoyment which he could experience only as a humiliation; he imagined himself—himself—humiliated by this passive voluptuousness, by this woman's sex" (p. 127).[16]

Malraux is aware that the sexual act does not in itself give a man true power over his partner. "Without love," he declares in *The Royal Way*, "there can be no possession" (p. 214). Nevertheless he generally associates sexual activity with the conquest and degradation of a woman.[17] He refers in *Man's Fate* to "the fundamental misogyny of almost all men," who feel entitled to despise a woman once she submits to their desires (p. 55). When the protagonist of this novel discovers that his wife has been to bed with another man, he is infuriated by the thought that her partner will now be able to speak of her with scorn despite his own awareness that her casual infidelity involved no emotional surrender on her part.

The tendency of Malraux's male characters to regard intercourse as an act of aggression against a woman is most strikingly illustrated by the terrorist, Ch'en, in *Man's Fate*. Returning to his comrades after committing his first murder, Ch'en suddenly sees them in a new light, as he had seen "his sister the first time he had come back from a brothel" (p. 18). When Ch'en confides that he has just killed a man, Gisors asks about his sexual history. Ch'en acknowledges that

Gisors's implied comparison is appropriate, since one despises the man one kills. After his first sexual experience, Ch'en declares, he felt a sense of pride less at being a man than at not being a woman.[18]

MALRAUX'S first novel-length work, *The Temptation of the West*, is composed of letters exchanged by two young men, A. D., a Frenchman visiting China, and Ling, a Chinese visiting Europe. Through these letters Malraux reveals his own dissatisfaction with traditional Western assumptions about the nature of the self. A. D.'s exposure to oriental culture leads him to question whether the self exists at all: "Western meditations on the subject have always accorded the 'I' a state of permanence. That it is distinct from the universe is implicit in this position. The Chinese I have met do not accept this duality at all, and I must admit that it holds little sway over me. However hard I try to be conscious of myself, I sense only a chaotic series of sensations over which I have no command at all, and which are only dependent on my imagination and the responses it calls up."[19] The "chaotic series of sensations" that A. D. discovers within himself calls to mind the continuous flux that D. H. Lawrence equates with a vital existence. But while Lawrence regards ever-changing impulse as the basis of genuine identity, Malraux suggests that man's lack of internal consistency challenges the very notion of an intrinsic self.

Finding that introspection fails to reveal a coherent sense of personal identity, A. D. concludes that the subjective impression of selfhood that most of us possess is only a vague fantasy of unspecified powers. In order to preserve a gratifying sense of unlimited potentiality, we avoid defining ourselves in any meaningful way:

One of the most important single elements of our lives [is] that awareness we have of ourselves which is so veiled, so opposed to reason that any attempt of the mind to understand it only makes it disappear. Nothing definite, nothing that allows us to define ourselves; only a sort of latent power . . . As if we lacked only the opportunity to carry out in the real world the exploits of our dreams, we retain the confused impression, not of having accomplished them, but of having been capable of accomplishing them. We are aware of this power within us just as an athlete, without thinking about it, is conscious of his strength. Pitiable actors who don't want to stop playing our glorious roles, we are, in our own eyes, creatures in whom is dormant an unsophisticated and jumbled procession of the possibilities of act and dream.

In this kind of consciousness, sustained, with the promises or hopes of human life, by all the riches of delirium, being cannot lower itself to becoming: being *someone*. (P. 52)

While Lawrence argues that any attempt to formulate a fixed idea of oneself can lead only to a distortion of one's nature, Malraux suggests that a commitment to a specific sense of identity is a prerequisite of authentic selfhood.[20]

While contact with the Orient makes the European skeptical of Western assumptions about the self, exposure to Western individualism challenges the Oriental's traditional belief that the self is not a discrete entity but an integral part of the universe. Ling is deeply pessimistic about the impact of Western thought upon China's future. He writes to A. D. that those of his countrymen who come into contact with the Occident become "barren of their own culture, disgusted with yours . . . The individual is being born in them, and with him that strange, passionless desire for destruction and anarchy" (p. 112). A. D. is equally pessimistic about the future of the West. In his final letter to Ling he observes, "In order to destroy God, and after having destroyed Him, Western intellect has abolished all which might have stood in the path of Man: having reached the limit of its efforts, it finds only death'' (p. 121). At the time he wrote this book Malraux apparently believed that individualistic humanism was about to destroy both the East and the West. The Oriental who comes into contact with Western thought becomes burdened with a self that has no role within his culture, and he can assert his new-found individuality only through senseless violence. The Occidental, having cut himself off from both God and the universe in his effort to make man the measure of all things, finds that the values he sacrificed in the name of humanity were precisely what had made man's life worthwhile. Paradoxically the Oriental, made restless by his discovery of selfhood, reaches the brink of violent action just as the Occidental, grown weary of the self he has worshipped for so long, sinks into passive lethargy. ''Unstable image of myself,'' A. D. writes, ''I love you not at all . . . I have given you everything, and still I know that I shall never love you. Without bowing down, each day I shall bring you peace as an offering'' (pp. 121-122).

THERE is a striking difference between the views expressed in *The Temptation of the West* and the attitudes that inform Malraux's subsequent novels. During the two years between the publication of *The Temptation of the West* and *The Conquerors* Malraux became convinced that certain values can be affirmed despite the death of God. [21] Stripped of the beliefs that had sustained earlier generations, A. D. at the end of *The Temptation of the West* is left a passive supplicant before ''voracious lucidity,'' his only remaining value. In Malraux's next two works, however, the protagonists' conviction that human existence lacks intrinsic meaning leads not to passivity but to action. Both Garine in *The Conquerors* and Perken in *The Royal Way* are quintessentially Nietzschean figures, set apart from common men by the strength of their will to power. But because it is narrower in scope, *The Royal Way* focuses more sharply than *The Conquerors* on an individual's struggle to create a chosen self in the face of an absurd universe.

Perken denies placing a higher value on being than on doing: "Just to *be* a king means nothing; it's the building up of a kingdom that's worth while" (p. 73). But his activity has no intrinsic value. The military force he struggles to create would have little worth in his eyes if he were not its creator; if his efforts fail, little will be lost except his self-esteem. Perken thus pursues an identity that rests upon achievement, but the sole purpose of his achievement is the creation of this identity. Malraux has apparently not yet formulated the clear-cut distinction between being and doing as motives for action that will be so important in *Man's Hope*, for he does not encourage us to question Perken's view of the significance of his endeavors.

Each of the major characters in *The Royal Way* emphasizes his difference from other men. Grabot is described as a man who has "never given a thought to anything except himself, or, more exactly, the side of his character which makes him a man apart" (p. 125). Priding himself on his solitary rebellion, Perken declares, "D' you see all those damn-fool insects making for our lamp, obeying the call of the light? The termites, too, obey the law of the anthill. I . . . *I will not obey*" (p. 142). Even on the verge of death he remains convinced of his uniqueness: "No man had ever *died;* all had but drifted into nothingness like the smokeclouds yonder dissolving into air, like the forest and the temples. He, only he, would die, be wrenched out of the scheme of things" (pp. 246-247).

Claude, too, is eager to prove himself an extraordinary man. His decision to stay with the dying Perken at the risk of losing his treasure reinforces his sense of superiority to the common run of men: "The strength of their fellow-feeling, unsuspected until now, struck him as a revelation. And was it not by sudden resolutions of this kind, and by them alone, that he could foster the contempt which separated him from the conventions and compromises of the herd?" (p. 210).[22]

The kind of identification that unites Claude with Perken provides Malraux's early protagonists with their only escape from total isolation. Referring to both *The Conquerors* and *The Royal Way,* Geoffrey Hartman observes, "The younger man absorbs the experience of the older and becomes, potentially, his redemptive double. If fate imposes anonymity, Man aspires to synonymity."[23] While the central characters in these novels, like earlier Romantic outsiders, define themselves in opposition to the rest of mankind, their sense of a unique identity that sets them apart from all others paradoxically needs validation by a figure resembling themselves.

In *The Mortal No* Frederick J. Hoffman identifies modern man's preoccupation with death as the starting point of his efforts at self-definition: "The self must choose what he is, what he will be, what he will do by way of assuming a position with respect to his death."[24] Few novels corroborate this point of view more emphatically than *The Royal Way.* Human mortality is the central preoccupation of the youthful Claude as well as the aging Perken, both of whom view their lives as a perpetual battle against the power of death.[25] Their paradoxical attitude toward human existence is reflected in two statements occurring only six pages apart: "To be a living man was even more absurd than dying!" (p. 243) and yet, "No hope of heaven, no promise of reward, nothing can justify the end of any human life!'' (p. 249). Death is to be abhorred not because it terminates a life that is intrinsically valuable, but because, by its very existence, it renders that life absurd.[26] Perken declares, ''You know as well as I do that life is meaningless; when a man lives alone he can't help brooding over the problem of his destiny. And death is always there, you see, ahead of him, like . . . like a standing proof of the futility of life'' (pp. 141-142).

The aspect of man's fate that is most central to this novel is not simply mortality, but the inescapable knowledge that one must die.[27] To seek a safe existence, avoiding every risk in an effort to forestall an inevitable end is, Malraux suggests, a lifelong submission to the power of death. By boldly confronting danger, Perken and Claude attempt to repudiate this power: ''But, living, to endure the vanity of life gnawing him [Claude] like a cancer; all his life long to feel the sweat of death lie clammy on his palm . . . unbearable! . . . What was his quest of the unknown, the slave's brief spell of freedom from his master, that men who do not understand it call adventure—what was it but his counter attack on death?'' (pp. 44-45). While self-preservation requires the ransom of constant caution, indifference toward life deprives death of its hostage. Grabot at one time claimed to possess the freedom that only such indifference can confer: ''And, as I don't give a hoot whether I croak or not—what's more, I rather like the idea of it—things can go as they damn well choose. If they go badly, they can't go any further than the muzzle of my revolver'' (pp. 126-127). But even before we learn of his ultimate fate, we are encouraged to question Grabot's assumption that suicide is always within man's power. ''Quite possibly it's no harder to die for oneself—in one's own interest, I mean—than to live for oneself; but I'm not so sure about it,'' Perken declares. ''Obviously it's up to a man to kill himself when he feels he's wearing out, but that's the very time when he starts loving life again" (p. 128).[28] When Grabot is finally found, he proves to be a blind, shackled slave. The impulse to survive no less than the capacity to die renders human volition powerless in the face of destiny.

Grabot's determination to exist only on his own terms is mocked by his actual behavior. Perken, on the other hand, apparently succeeds in treating his own life as "so much raw material," resisting until the moment of his death any involuntary impulse that would undermine his chosen identity. Like Julien Sorel, Perken is among those literary characters who, in Malraux's words, "accomplish premeditated acts in accordance with a general conception of life."[29] Yet Malraux's depiction of Perken, like Stendhal's portrayal of Julien, does not eliminate the possibility of psychological determinism, but merely pushes it behind the scenes.

The limits of conscious volition are suggested in the opening pages of *The Royal Way*. During a discussion of erotic desire Perken compares the imagination to "a foreign body lodged inside us, yet a part of ourselves for all that" (p. 4). A short while later he adds, "A man ekes out his imagination as best he can, not as he chooses" (p. 7). Later Perken identifies his own sexual desires with his martial ambitions: "You see, I want to survive for many men, and perhaps for a long time; to leave my mark upon the map of Asia. In the great game I'm playing against death I'd rather have twenty tribes to back me than a child . . . Yes, that was what I wanted, just as my father coveted his neighbor's land—or I want women" (p. 74). This analogy between Perken's desires for power and for women suggests that if his erotic tastes are beyond the domain of his will, so is his dedication to adventure.

The question of whether Perken's pursuit of danger is truly a matter of choice is made even more problematic by his response to the prospect of pain. Malraux apparently intends us to share Perken's belief that his readiness to risk torture is motivated solely by a conscious desire to realize his conception of himself. Many years after writing *The Royal Way* Malraux described Perken as a Prometheus-like figure whose courageous defiance constitutes a symbolic triumph for mankind:

> The book and the character arose from a speculation on what man can do against death. Whence this prototype of the hero without a cause, ready to risk torture simply for the sake of his own conception of himself, and perhaps for a kind of blinding perception of his destiny—because the risk of torture alone seems to him to triumph over death . . . the man who accepts the risk of torture—even if *only* for his own arbitrary conception of himself and, more deeply, for a cause which is not the defense of his own kin but the human condition—does not commit himself alone . . . or his near ones, like the traditional hero, but the human condition, like Prometheus.[30]

But Malraux's actual depiction of Perken suggests not a stoical acceptance of torture as the necessary price of freedom, but a compulsive pursuit of pain rationalized as a rebellion against death. Thus Perken's readiness to risk torture in the name of his convictions, like that of many more conventional martyrs, gives considerable evidence of being more pathological than heroic.[31]

The thought of undergoing the worst torments he can imagine fills Perken with a strange elation:

> A grotesque notion flashed across his mind—of the punishments assigned to Pride—a vision of himself with mangled, twisted limbs, head lolling backwards like a shouldered pack, and his body like a stake driven into the earth. He felt an insensate long-

ing that such torments should exist, so that, in their extremity, a man might be enabled to spit in the face of torture, and defy it with full consciousness, with all his will, though it should make him shriek with agony. And such was his wild elation at the thought that he was risking more than death, so vividly did he see it as his revenge upon the universe, his warrant of release from man's estate, that he was conscious of an inward struggle, an effort to fight down an overpowering hallucination, a kind of ecstasy. (Pp. 176-177)[32]

The prospect of enduring the unendurable is the one stimulus that can destroy Perken's self-possession, making his behavior wholly independent of his will: a "driving force that urged him like a fascinated animal" impels him toward his torturers (p. 178). Upon being rescued from danger, Perken experiences "hatred of mankind, of life, of all the forces that were mastering him again and scattering the wild memories of that terrific moment, like the lost splendor of a vision" (p. 192).

Although Grabot remains a shadowy figure throughout *The Royal Way,* he, too, exemplifies the difficulty of distinguishing between the freely willed and the psychologically fated. Because he has far more difficulty than Perken in reconciling his conscious self-image with his erotic needs, he provides an even more striking demonstration of the power of the unconscious. Since Perken's need for sexual "conquest" is in harmony with his general conception of himself, he is never forced to acknowledge any source of his behavior except his conscious will. On the other hand, Grabot's desire "to have a woman tie him up, naked, for an hour or so in a dark room" (p. 8) makes it impossible to attribute his entire mode of existence to a chosen image of himself. Perken regards the foolhardy defiance characteristic of Grabot's life as a means of compensating for his humiliating sexual needs. But although Grabot himself presumably views his behavior as evidence of virile courage, his actions (sacrificing his own eye in order to get revenge on a military doctor who refused to grant him sick leave, deliberately subjecting himself to the excruciatingly painful sting of the black scorpion, and allowing himself to be almost eaten alive by ants) follow a consistent pattern that suggests not aggressive self-assertion but masochistic self-destructiveness. Self-mutilation (particularly by injury to the eye) is viewed by many psychologists as a means of symbolic castration.[33] Thus Grabot's repeated acts of self-punishment suggest the same repudiation of masculinity that is reflected in his erotic practices. The compulsive nature of Grabot's pursuit of danger is apparent even to Perken, who observes, "He finds the same pleasure that we all do in risking our lives, but for him the pleasure's all the keener because it's more essential to him" (p. 127). Like the destruction of his eye and his encounter with the scorpion, Grabot's single-handed confrontation with the Mois would appear to be a self-destructive action disguised as self-assertion. Having progressed from prostitutes' ropes to infected eyes to scorpion bites, Grabot finally finds himself irresistibly drawn toward the legendary cruelty of the Mois, at whose hands the darkness and bondage he once sought in brothels becomes his permanent fate.[34] Certain aspects of Grabot's history recall that of Gerald Crich, who at one time pursued an existence similar to his as an explorer of the Amazon. Repressing his deepest desires more fully than Grabot, Gerald manifests his unconscious wish for restraint in a conscious dread of being bound hand and foot. But like Grabot he prides himself on the power of his will while in fact longing to be dominated and finally destroyed.

Perken's ultimate fate, like Grabot's, bears a striking resemblance to his earlier masochistic fantasies, which in his case involved not blindness and passivity but lucidity and self-control. Fatally wounded by a poisoned war spike, he scornfully refuses to ease his suffering with opium and dies with his will intact, fully conscious of excruciating pain. Denying death's existence as a force outside himself, his final words declare him to be not a passive victim but an agent of his destiny: "There is . . . no death. There's only . . . I . . . I who . . . am dying" (pp. 249-250).[35]

Malraux apparently intends *The Royal Way* as a Byronic tribute to the human will, "Triumphant where it dares defy,/ And making Death a Victory." But Byron can succeed in making characters like Prometheus and Manfred symbolize the power of conscious volition only because he portrays them on a mythic rather than a human scale. Malraux, on the other hand, never allows his respect for the heroic to override his perception of the human. His admiration for the metaphysical rebel at war with the human condition does not prevent him from depicting such a man in his full complexity, even if his portrait ultimately suggests that human freedom is circumscribed by forces within the psyche as well as by those without. At one point in the novel Malraux in fact suggests that Perken's very determination to triumph over death is the product of a self-destructive impulse: "What [Perkin is] really after, Claude mused, is self-annihilation. I wonder is he more aware of it than he admits" (p. 77). But except for this casual remark Malraux devotes no attention to the possibility of psychological compulsion masquerading as deliberate choice.[36] Not until *Man's Fate,* his next and greatest novel, does he come to grips with the disturbing realization that the conscious will may itself constitute an instrument of internal fatality.

EXISTENTIALISM in its most radical form denies the existence of psychological causality, defining man simply as the sum of his freely chosen acts. Malraux's emphasis on man's capacity to act in accordance with his conscious values has led some readers to identify him with this perspective.[37] On at least two occasions, however, Malraux has explicitly repudiated this reductionistic view of the self. Responding to a critic's reference to an assertion by one of his characters that man is not what he hides but what he achieves, Malraux declared, "He does say that without contradiction, but a great deal might have been said in response . . . Because if man is not what he hides, neither is he only what he does." And in *Anti-Memoirs* Malraux writes: "A remark of one of my characters has been attributed to me: 'A man is what he does.' Of course he is not only that; the character was in any case replying to another who had just said: 'What is a man? A miserable little pile of secrets.' "[38]

Malraux's writings suggest that human behavior is generally deliberate rather than impulsive. But although his characters usually act in accordance with their conscious beliefs, Malraux does not go so far as to assume, as Sartre does, that each individual can freely choose the values that will prompt his choice of action.[39] For Malraux, therefore, an individual's personal convictions are likely to constitute an internal compulsion that restricts him to a particular way of life. W. M. Frohock has aptly observed that in Malraux's novels a given character acts "*as he is forced to* by his attitude toward death, sex, human dignity, power, liberty, or something similar" (italics mine).[40]

In *Man's Fate* Malraux shows a variety of ideas taking the form of obsessive drives. The character whose motives are most fully explored is Ch'en, the young Chinese whose need for an absolute of some kind makes him a dedicated terrorist.

Educated as a Christian, Ch'en rejected his religion shortly after leaving a Lutheran college. But two aspects of his former faith have a lasting effect upon him. A Christian sense of the significance of the individual leads him "to isolate himself from the world instead of submitting to it" (p. 69), and his mentor's belief in the depravity of man's physical nature discloses to him a hell "more terrible and more convincing than the one he had been supposedly forewarned against" (p. 68). Ch'en's exposure to Western thought leaves him appalled by the merely human, even in the absence of the divine. He is alienated from the natural world yet incapable of transcending it: "What good is a soul," reflects Gisors, "if there is neither God nor Christ?" (p. 69).[41]

The sketch of Ch'en's biography provided in *Man's Fate,* brief as it is, gives us a kind of insight into the formative influences of a character's life that we rarely find in Malraux's novels. In *The Royal Way* Malraux had implicitly denied psychological causality by encouraging us to believe that the facts of Perken's biography are irrelevant to his identity at the time of his final adventure: "Perken's early history . . . simply did not exist; so *real* was he, standing there, that the things he had done fell from him, like idle dreams. Of the 'facts' of Perken's life Claude would accept none but those which tallied with his vision of the man" (p. 32). The omission of all details about Perken's former life is one means by which Malraux tries to convince us that he is truly a free agent whose present behavior has no source beyond his autonomous will. On the other hand, by suggesting that religious influences deeply affected Ch'en's response to life, Malraux points to a causal relationship between past and present, indicating that Ch'en's will has itself been conditioned by external circumstances.

To be a mere man in a world without God is unbearable to

Ch'en. The act of killing gives him a sense of transcending ordinary human existence, "the life of men who do not kill." He regards murder as a supreme act of self-assertion that permits him to despise not only his victim but all "weaklings" who dare not do as he has done. And yet he seems to suspect that the murder he commits is not a freely chosen act but a product of internal compulsion: "Ch'en was becoming aware, with a revulsion verging on nausea, that he stood here, not as a fighter, but as a sacrificial priest. [And not only to the gods of his choice];[42] but beneath his sacrifice to the Revolution lay a world of depths beside which this night of crushing anguish was bright as day" (p. 10). Ch'en later suggests that his own terrorist activities, in appearance the ultimate exercise of anarchistic individualism, are paradoxically analogous to the obedience of the disciplined party member: "[It's the same for this fellow Vologin,][43] I guess; but for him, instead of murder, it's obedience. For people who live as we do there must be a certainty. For him, carrying out orders is sure, I suppose, as killing is for me. Something *must* be sure. Must be" (p. 156).[44] At this point Ch'en seems to recognize that he is driven to violence by his fear of the uncertainty that is a concomitant of freedom. But in spite of his insight into his own compulsive needs, Ch'en remains convinced that his suicidal attempt on Chiang Kai-shek's life will constitute a freely chosen act. Both Gisors and Kyo recognize, however, that Ch'en's behavior is a product of internal necessity. When Ch'en speaks to Gisors about his first murder, Gisors immediately suspects that what Ch'en really wants above all is to die (p. 65). Later Kyo perceives the compulsive nature of Ch'en's determination to assassinate Chiang: "Indeed, Kyo felt that Ch'en's will in the matter played a very small role. If destiny lived somewhere, it was there tonight, by his side'' (p. 159).[45]

Two of the most sophisticated of Malraux's critics have reached opposite conclusions about the meaning of Ch'en's behavior. According to Geoffrey Hartman, Ch'en attempts to assert his freedom through an act he is fated to perform: "Tchen becomes a tragic figure when his own act questions him, not as an individual or as a murderer, but as everyman who must convert some fatality into a purely human act of will."[46] In a review of Hartman's book Neal Oxenhandler argues that Malraux's characters do not try to convert fatality into freedom but, on the contrary, to convert an act of will into a fatality as they strive to raise themselves "from existence to being, from the level of the contingent to the necessary."[47] Both analyses are in fact valid. Unable to bear the burden of freedom that is man's lot in a world without God, Ch'en denies the contingent nature of all human enterprise by attributing absolute value to revolutionary terrorism. But he also insists that his acts of terrorism prove the power of his will. In actuality, however, his very need to escape from universal contingency leads to an obsession with violence that precludes true freedom of choice.

Gerda Blumenthal compares Ch'en throwing himself joyfully upon Chiang Kai-shek's car with Perken ecstatically approaching the Mois. Both "experience their orgiastic descent into the private subterranean palace of dreams and obsessions as a culmination of deliverance. What seems to them the assertion of an absolute freedom is in fact the total consent of the fatalist to being imprisoned in the closed cycle of eternal recurrence."[48] There is indeed a similarity in the behavior of these two characters, but an important change has occurred in Malraux's conception of the behavior he describes. In *The Royal Way* he appears on the whole to share Perken's view of the significance of his actions. But in *Man's Fate* he clearly indicates that Ch'en's preoccupation with the power of his "free" will is itself an internal compulsion.

Clappique and Ferral are, like Ch'en, paradoxically impelled to act as they do by the idea of their own freedom. Assuming themselves devoid of an intrinsic, determining nature, they each become obsessed with the notion of self-creation. Finding within himself no basis for claiming a fixed identity, Clappique claims to be the "only man in Shanghai who does not exist" (p. 206). To compensate for the authentic self that he lacks, Clappique proliferates fictional versions of his identity. His imaginary selves, the product of mere words, appear to possess a certain reality for him as long as they are validated by the credulity of a listener. Clappique believes himself free from any fixed mode of existence, but Gisors interprets his continual masquerade as a response to a persistent emotional need: "His mythomania is a means of denying life . . . Everything has happened as though he wanted to prove to himself this evening that, although he lived for two hours like a rich man, wealth does not exist. Because then *poverty does not exist either.* Which is essential. Nothing exists: all is dream" (p. 46). Although Clappique claims to possess no consistent characteristics, his very irresponsibility becomes an identifying trait. When he fails to collect the money that has been promised to him, Kyo observes that "each time Clappique behaved in this way he was so much himself that he only half surprised those who knew him" (p. 265).

When Clappique disguises himself as a sailor in order to

escape from Shanghai, he believes he has found a way of actually realizing one of his fictional selves: "He had found, suddenly, by accident, the most dazzling success of his life. No, men do not exist, since a costume is enough to enable one to escape from oneself, to find another life in the eyes of others. It was the same feeling of strangeness, of happiness that had seized him the first time he had found himself in a Chinese crowd—but now the sensation had not only surface, but depth. 'Now I'm living a story, not merely telling one!' " (p. 313). But Clappique's notion of "living a story" does not seem to involve much of a departure from his habitual behavior. Finding a willing listener, he immediately embarks upon a highly improbable narrative in precisely his former manner.[49]

Acknowledging no relation between behavior and identity, Clappique contentedly accepts his own "nonexistence" and retreats into a world of fantasy. Ferral, on the other hand, feels obliged to affirm his existence through a continual effort of will. An obsessive need to create his own identity underlies not only Ferral's commercial activities, but his erotic and intellectual life as well. His powerful position offers him an obvious basis for self-definition, but he refuses to be equated with the office he holds: "He did not want to be merely the President of the Consortium, he wanted to be distinct from his activity—a way of considering himself superior to it. His almost aggressive love of art, of thought, of the cynicism which he called lucidity, was a defense" (p. 237). Despite this desire to be "distinct from his activity," Ferral can ultimately define himself only in terms of the impact of his actions upon the external world. Erotic and industrial achievements provide him with two alternative props for his ego.

Women become essential to him when he doubts his power in the financial world. A feeling of helplessness before uncontrollable economic forces drives him to Valérie's bedroom:

> Would he, all his life, never be able to do more than wait, in order to take advantage of them, for the passage of those great tidal sweeps of world economy that began like offerings and ended like blows below the belt? Tonight, in case of either resistance, victory or defeat, he felt himself dependent upon all the forces of the world. But there was this woman upon whom he did not depend, who would presently depend on him; the avowal of submission on her face at the moment of possession, like a hand plastered over his eyes, would conceal from him the network of constraints on which his life rested. (P. 226)

But when Valérie humiliates Ferral in revenge for his treatment of her, he no longer wants to perceive himself through his mistress's eyes. The need for a conception of his identity in which women play no part leads to his often-quoted Existential manifesto: "Man can and must deny woman: action, action alone justifies life and satisfies the white man. What would we think if we were told of a painter who makes no paintings? A man is the sum of his actions, of what he has *done,* of what he can do. Nothing else. I am not what such and such an encounter with a man or woman may have done to shape my life; I am my roads, my . . ." (pp. 241-242). This definition of selfhood does not, however, fully satisfy Ferral, who "needed the eyes of others to see himself, the senses of another to feel himself" (p. 245). A few pages after his conversation with Gisors he is once more demonstrating his prowess in a woman's bed, the only place that he can find assurance of his power: "He went to women to be judged, he who countenanced no judgment" (pp. 243-244). The necessity of perpetual self-creation proves to be an exhausting burden that Ferral can escape only when he abdicates consciousness itself: "He had lived, fought, created; beneath all those appearances, deep down, he found this to be the only reality, the joy of abandoning himself, of leaving upon the shore, like the body of a drowned companion, that creature, himself, whose life it was necessary each day to invent anew. 'To sleep is the only thing I have always really wanted, for so many years'" (p. 244).

Impelled to a ceaseless pursuit of power by his desire to achieve a chosen self, Ferral has much in common with the heroes of Malraux's two preceding novels. But these works suggest that determined action is intrinsically admirable independent of its goal. Garine's assertion that all that is not revolution is worse than revolution cannot stamp out the reader's suspicion that he has chosen his cause almost at random, and Perken's political involvement is given no moral significance. (The question of responsibility for the native deaths resulting from his activities is never raised.) By the time of writing *Man's Fate* Malraux has come to believe that even in an absurd universe human activity can be directed toward a worthwhile goal. Perken epitomizes man pitted against the inhuman, and we are encouraged to admire rather than judge him. But in *Man's Fate,* where men are pitted against men, moral judgments become relevant. In the context of *The Royal Way* individualistic self-absorption leads to a heroic defiance of destiny; in the context of *Man's Fate* it results in a brutal indifference to one's fellows. The metaphysical struggle dramatized in *The Royal Way* is necessarily a solitary one, for human fraternity can have no impact upon an indifferent universe. But in Malraux's subsequent novels solidarity becomes a meaningful way to affirm human dignity in the face of injustice and oppression.

IN *Man's Fate* the elder Gisors, gifted with special insight into a world of action from which he remains aloof, often plays a role analogous to that of the narrator of the traditional novel, providing a framework for interpreting the behavior of other characters. Like Malraux himself, Gisors interprets virtually all human activity as an attempt to escape from the anguish of being a man. But he suggests two very different means of pursuing this fundamental goal. On the one hand he postulates a universal attempt to escape from the self through some form of intoxication:

> "It is very rare for a man to be able to endure—how shall I say it?—his condition, his fate as a man . . .
>
> There is always a need for intoxication: this country has opium, Islam has hashish, the West has woman . . . Perhaps love is above all the means which the Occidental uses to free himself from man's fate . . . "
>
> Under his words flowed an obscure and hidden counter-current of figures: Ch'en and murder, Clappique and his madness, Katov and the Revolution, May and love, himself and opium. (P. 241)

A short while later, however, he speaks of a universal longing to raise the self to the level of a god through assertion of the individual will:

> Men are perhaps indifferent to power . . . What fascinates them in this idea, you see, is not real power, it's the illusion of being able to do exactly as they please. The king's power is the power to govern, isn't it? But man has no urge to govern: he has an urge to compel, as you said. To be more than a man, in a world of men. To escape man's fate, I was saying. Not powerful: all-powerful. The visionary disease, of which the will to power is only the intellectual justification, is the will to god-head: every man dreams of being god. (P. 242)

The two means of circumventing the human condition that Gisors identifies here—escape from the will through "intoxication" and apotheosis of the will through the dream of godhead—correspond to the two conflicting impulses that so frequently coexist in earlier Romantic literature (see chapter 1, note 10). Gisors himself makes no attempt to reconcile these opposing desires. But throughout *Man's Fate* Malraux repeatedly demonstrates not only their coexistence within a single individual, but their simultaneous fulfillment by means of a single act. In very different ways Ch'en, Clappique, and Ferral pursue a common goal—the "self-possession" that will give them a feeling of omnipotence accompanied by a sense of being totally subject to the very will that they assert.

Inherent in the human condition is the fact that man does not have the power to control every aspect of his being. Suicide alone can bring an individual's entire existence within the scope of his will: thus volition can become absolute only at the cost of its destruction. Ch'en is obsessively drawn to such an apotheosis of the will. Self-inflicted death suggests to him "the complete possession of oneself. Total. Absolute. To know. Not to be looking, looking, always, for ideas, for duties. In the last hour I have felt nothing of what used to weigh on me. Do you hear? Nothing . . . I possess myself. But I don't feel a menace, an anguish, as always before. Possessed, held tight, tight, as this hand holds the other" (p. 196). In fact, Ch'en never actually attains his moment of self-possession.[50] During his last instant of consciousness he submits to the brutality of a policeman, and his actual death results from an involuntary reflex: "A furious kick from another officer caused all his muscles to contract: he fired without being aware of it" (p. 249).

The act of suicide transforms Ch'en's will into a destiny to which he must submit. Clappique finds in gambling a less fatal means of attaining a similar end. Malraux makes this analogy explicit: "He was discovering that gambling is a suicide without death: all he had to do was to place his money there, to look at the ball and wait, as he would have waited after having swallowed poison; a poison endlessly renewed, together with the pride of taking it" (p. 259). Choosing to stake his money (and indirectly both Kyo's life and his own) at the gambling table gives Clappique a sense of determining his fate by an act of will. At the same time, powerless to influence the movements of the ball upon which his future rests, he feels himself totally subject to forces beyond his control: "That ball which was slowing down was a destiny—*his* destiny. He was not struggling with a creature, but with a kind of god; and this god, at the same time, was himself" (p. 257). Clappique chooses to submit to chance, then apotheosizes the will that consents to this submission, much as Ch'en apotheosizes the will that consents to his death. Gambling represents to Clappique precisely what suicide does to Ch'en —"the only means he had ever found of possessing himself" (p. 258).

Ferral finds in eroticism the same sense of being simultaneously all-powerful and totally subject that Ch'en seeks through suicide and Clappique discovers while gambling. Through his identification with the woman he conquers he imagines himself to be helpless before his own will: "It was from his need to imagine himself in her place as soon as he began to touch her body that he derived his acute feeling of possession" (p. 227).[51] Ferral's will, like Ch'en's and Clappique's, ultimately turns inward upon the self: "But if he had never in his life possessed a single woman, he had possessed, he would possess through this Chinese woman who

was awaiting him, the only thing he was eager for: himself''
(p. 245).

Ferral's longing to ''possess'' himself is no less obsessive
than Ch'en's and Clappique's, but theirs involves a self-
destructive element that his seems to lack. Even before Ch'en
resolves to kill himself, both Gisors and Kyo suspect that a
suicidal impulse underlies his fascination with death. And
Clappique, we are told, is composed of two beings, ''the one
who wanted to live and the one who wanted to be destroyed''
(p. 257). In both Ch'en and Clappique the need for self-
assertion is relatively superficial, and at the moment of ''self-
possession'' they prove to be less possessor than possessed.
But Ferral's erotic needs require that he actually play an assertive role, experiencing only vicariously the passive acquiescence of his partner. Too successful in using others as objects
for his aggression to be a candidate for suicide, Ferral is, in
fact, one of the few characters in Malraux's novels wholly
committed to self-preservation. But in one respect Ferral too
is a victim of the need to ''possess'' himself, for the impulse
to degrade a woman dominates his sexual life and precludes
an affectionate relationship: ''The woman who would have
admired him in the giving of herself, whom he would not
have had to fight, would not have existed in his eyes,'' and
he is therefore condemned ''to coquettes or to whores'' (p.
244).

IF actions that are subjectively perceived as freely chosen can
be recognized by others as compulsive, can one ever be certain that his own will is free? Kyo's observation of Ch'en
leads him to suspect not: ''Is it only the fatality of others that
one sees, never one's own?'' he wonders (p. 166). Malraux's
depiction of Ch'en, Clappique, and Ferral implies that when

its ultimate goal is self-possession, the will is not an agent of man's freedom, but a pawn of his obsessions. In his portrayal of Kyo, however, Malraux suggests that man can exercise genuine freedom when he is committed to a cause beyond the self. The difference between Kyo's revolutionary activity, which is determined solely by ideological convictions, and Ch'en's, which is motivated by complex psychological needs, is made explicit early in the novel:

> Everything had pushed [Ch'en] into political activity: the hope of a different world, the possibility of eating, though wretchedly . . . the gratification of his hatreds, his mind, his character. This activity gave a meaning to his solitude.
>
> But with Kyo everything was simpler. The heroic sense had given him a kind of discipline, not a kind of justification of life. He was not restless. His life had a meaning, and he knew what it was: to give to each of these men whom famine, at this very moment, was killing off like a slow plague, the sense of his own dignity. (P. 70)

In *The Royal Way,* as in *The Red and the Black,* a pattern of behavior that suggests internal compulsion conflicts with the protagonist's claim to a freely created self. In *Man's Fate,* however, Malraux avoids such ambiguity by letting one protagonist illustrate the power of psychological compulsion while another exemplifies the truly autonomous will. Malraux's opposition of Kyo and Ch'en is thus closely analogous to Lawrence's contrast of Birkin and Gerald. Both Birkin and Kyo are exemplary characters who represent their creator's conception of genuine freedom, which to Lawrence means unrestrained spontaneity and to Malraux, volitional self-creation.

On the other hand, Gerald and Ch'en are each subject to internal compulsions that determine their way of life. The two characters who are free both perceive that their companions are not. Birkin observes a "strange sense of fatality" in Gerald (*Women in Love*, p. 199); and Kyo, walking beside Ch'en, senses that if "destiny lived somewhere, it was there tonight, by his side" (*Man's Fate*, p. 159). Both Gerald and Ch'en are characterized by an obsessive willfulness that masks a death wish, and both are ultimately drawn to suicide. Their behavior reveals underlying motivational patterns that invite psychological analysis. Connections are suggested between their past and present lives, and their personal histories help us understand their deepest emotional needs. On the other hand, we know nothing about the early life of either Birkin or Kyo, for any attempt to relate their present beliefs or actions to events that occurred in their past would undermine our impression of their freedom.

KYO is portrayed both as a dedicated revolutionary and as a private individual involved in a marital crisis. But Malraux does not share Lawrence's belief that a "radically unchanged element" underlies all seeming contradictions within the self, and the two halves of Kyo's life are not intended to be mutually illuminating. In fact, the discontinuity between Kyo's public and private existence is central to Malraux's conception of him: "Individual problems existed for Kyo only in his private life" (p. 70). While Kyo's political identity is wholly a product of volition, his marriage involves a part of him that is independent of his will.

Through his portrayal of the relationships between Ferral and Valérie on the one hand and Kyo and May on the other, Malraux implies a fundamental contrast between eroticism and love. The male enters an erotic relationship, Malraux suggests, to find reflected in his partner's eyes an identity that he creates through deliberate actions. Two people in

143

love, however, find in each other the affirmation of a self that is not defined by one's acts. "To May alone, [Kyo] was not what he had done; to him alone, she was something altogether different from her biography . . . Since his mother had died, May was the only being for whom he was not Kyo Gisors, but an intimate partner . . . 'Men are not my kind, they are those who look at me and judge me; my kind are those who love me and do not look at me, who love me in spite of everything, degradation, baseness, treason—*me* and not what I have done or shall do—who would love me as long as I would love myself' " (p. 59).

The self that is the object of an intimate partner's love ("*me* and not what I have done or shall do") has an extremely problematic status for Malraux. In a somewhat obscure but highly significant passage he simultaneously denies the objective existence of this private self and affirms its subjective reality: "The embrace by which love holds beings together against solitude did not bring its relief to man; it brought relief only to the madman, to the incomparable monster, dear above all things, that every being is to himself and that he cherishes in his heart" (p. 59).[52]

When we see Kyo acting as a dedicated Communist, his feelings are in perfect accord with his convictions. But in the context of his relationship with May he is subject to emotions that have nothing to do with his consciously held beliefs. His theoretical acceptance of May's freedom does not mitigate his anguish when she tells him she went to bed with another man.[53] He can neither justify nor overcome the jealousy that torments him: "Kyo was suffering from the most humiliating pain: that which one despises oneself for feeling" (pp. 53-54). Distanced from May by his jealousy, Kyo is struck by a painful recognition of her difference from him: "The essential, what agonized him, was that he was suddenly sepa-

144

rated from her . . . And now this body was being invested with the poignant mystery of a familiar person suddenly transformed . . . And she was a woman. Not a kind of man. Something else" (pp. 55-56). According to D. H. Lawrence, recognition of the unknowable "otherness" of the opposite sex is a prerequisite for a healthy marriage. Malraux, on the other hand, views such recognition as the sign of a breach between husband and wife that both are powerless to mend. Kyo's alienation from May later leads him to refuse her the right to share his danger. This decision, like his jealousy itself, is the product of impulses that are counter to his consciously held values: "Kyo felt some familiar demons stirring within him, which rather thoroughly disgusted him. He had an urge to strike her, to strike directly at her love" (p. 213).

When Kyo finally decides to let May risk her life by his side, he experiences an unprecedented emotion: "He stopped, overwhelmed by the brotherhood of death, discovering how derisive the flesh appeared before this communion, in spite of its urgent appeal. He understood now that the willingness to lead the being one loves to death itself is perhaps the complete expression of love, that which cannot be surpassed" (p. 216). The "brotherhood of death" ("*la fraternité de la mort*") that Malraux encourages us to regard as the highest form of conjugal love would appear to have far more in common with the "virile fraternity" that he elsewhere attributes to men united by a cause than with the intimacy so central to Kyo's past relationship with May. However intense this new "brotherhood" may be, it proves shortlived indeed, for it survives only as long as they share the same relation to death. Once Kyo knows that he will die and May will continue to live, he again perceives her as a being distinctly separate from himself, a source of irrational guilt and even perhaps an object of involuntary resentment: "He would not see May again, and the only grief that left him vulnerable was her grief, as if his own death were a fault. 'The remorse of dying,' he thought with a contracted irony. No such feeling with regard to his father, who had always given him the impression not of weakness, but of strength" (pp. 321-322). Simultaneously wanting her to forget him and fearing that she will do so, he does not write to her because a farewell letter would have "attached her all the more to him" and also because "it would be telling her to love another" (p. 322). Kyo's proximity to death ineluctably separates him from the living. The "brotherhood of death" now unites him not with May but with the comrades who share his doom.

THE portrayal of Kyo as May's husband reflects Malraux's awareness of the complex, irrational motives that often determine human behavior. But the depiction of this same character as a revolutionary fighter suggests that an individual's private vulnerability need not undermine his capacity for purely volitional action on behalf of a chosen cause. Even after his capture Kyo's firm allegiance to his consciously held values makes him an embodiment of the self-creating will. Kyo regards his imminent death not as a defeat but as an affirmation of the commitment that gives meaning to his existence: "What would have been the value," he asks himself, "of a life for which he would not have been willing to die?" (p. 323). Having rejected an opportunity to save his own life by betraying his comrades, Kyo kills himself to avoid being tortured, facing death with the stoic self-possession that Ch'en longed in vain to achieve: "To die is passivity, but to kill oneself is action. As soon as they came to fetch the first of their group, he would kill himself with full consciousness" (p. 321). His suicide is described as a quintessential act of will: "He crushed the poison between his teeth as he would have given a command" (p.323).[54]

In *Anti-Memoirs* Malraux declares that the "metamorphosis of a fate undergone into a fate transcended is one of the most profound that man can create."[55] Dying on his own terms with his will intact, Kyo provides an example of man's capacity to effect such a metamorphosis. But the novel's greatest tribute to the strength of human volition is Katov's sacrifice of the very power to control the manner of his dying. Within the framework of Malraux's values the horror of torture is closely related to its power to wreak havoc with one's will. Chiang Kai-shek's police chief König is obsessed with self-disgust because he had once wept before his tormentors.[56] To be thus shorn of self-possession by unendurable pain is made to seem the most humiliating fate man can endure. But by deliberately choosing an agonizing death to spare men who are weaker than himself, Katov turns the most unbearable of fates into the ultimate victory of the conscious will over the vulnerability of the flesh.

The development of Malraux's concept of heroism between *The Royal Way* and *Man's Fate* becomes clear when we compare Katov's attitude immediately before his execution with Perken's when he confronts the Mois. Perken excites himself by imagining the excruciating tortures that supposedly await him. Katov, on the other hand, tries to reduce his imminent ordeal to the less terrifying aspect of mere accident: "Well! let's suppose I died in a fire" (p. 328). What matters to Katov is not the narcissistic pleasure of observing his own endurance, but the realization that no fear of pain can undermine his commitment to an ideal.

Although Katov's sacrifice would appear to constitute the novel's strongest affirmation of fraternity, he does not in fact share the gratifying sense of communion that helps Kyo face death. Katov's heroism does not result from a sense of oneness with his comrades, but from a determination to transcend his fear and isolation: "In spite of all these men who had fought as he had, Katov was alone, alone between the body of his dead friend and his two terror-stricken companions, alone between this wall and that whistle far off in the night. But a man could be stronger than this solitude and even, perhaps, than that atrocious whistle" (p. 325). Katov's immediate reward, a "pitiful fraternity, without a face, almost without a real voice," is shortlived, for as soon as his comrades make use of his gift of death, Katov, more alone than ever, "[feels] himself deserted" (p. 327). The real reward of his sacrifice, however, is not a brief moment of "pitiful fraternity," but the satisfaction of having proved man's power to transcend even the most appalling of fates.[57]

BOTH *The Royal Way* and *Women in Love* give exemplary status to individuals who repudiate all social ties in their pursuit of self-fulfillment.[58] Shortly after writing these novels Lawrence and Malraux each become dissatisfied with a system of values that deprives the individual of all communal bonds. In the next stage of their careers, both writers retain the critical view of their own society that previously led them to exalt such voluntary exiles as Birkin and Perken. Now, however, their ideal is not anarchic individualism, but a degree of social unity seldom found in the modern world. In his preface to *Days of Contempt* Malraux attacks the deliberate nonconformity that is as central to his own early novels as to any other literary works: "The history of artistic sensibility in France for the past fifty years might be called the death-agony of the brotherhood of man. Its real enemy is an unformulated individualism which . . . sprang less from the will to create a man whole than from a fanatical desire to be different . . . The individual stands in opposition to society, but he is nourished by it. And it is far less important to know what differentiates him than what nourishes him.''[59]

While paralleling each other in their movement from an individualistic to a communalist perspective, Lawrence and Malraux differ as greatly in their ideas about communion as in their definitions of the self. Their search for an alternative to individual isolation leads them to opposite ideologies: Lawrence's political novels espouse hierarchical order; Malraux's, Marxist revolution.[60] From a metaphysical as well as a political viewpoint their ideas could hardly be further apart. Assuming the natural scheme of things to be fundamentally good, Lawrence believes that man's deepest desires are invariably congruent with the destiny assigned to him by nature. In moving from an individualistic to a communalist system of values, he repudiates his earlier conviction that man is intrinsically "single" and concludes that we are inherently part of a larger whole. Malraux, on the other hand, believes that man's deepest desires are doomed to frustration by the human condition itself. Far from regarding individual isolation as a deviation from nature, he insists that the pain of solitude is intrinsic to man's fate.[61] But he also believes that certain individuals can at times transcend their inherent aloneness through love or fraternal union.

Although Lawrence's would appear to be the more optimistic perspective, human communion as an achieved reality rather than an ideal goal plays a far greater role in Malraux's than in Lawrence's works. In *Man's Fate,* for example, Malraux attributes to Kyo a sense of fraternity strong enough to conquer the fear of death: "[Kyo] was dying among those with whom he would have wanted to live; he was dying, like each of these men, because he had given a meaning to his life

. . . It is easy to die when one does not die alone'' (p. 323). Not all readers find this passage convincing. The skeptic's position is forcefully argued by Murray Krieger: "Surely without May this Kyo does die alone. His fellow prisoners cannot replace her, cannot break through to the private, subjective Kyo. It is only the public Kyo who can share with them; the Kyo who—a creature of Ferral's universe—is no more than the sum of his actions, 'what he has *done*'; the Kyo of the phonograph records, heard with the ears and not the throat."[62] The logic of Krieger's argument cannot, however, disprove the existence of a subjective sense of fraternity among strangers united by dedication to a cause. Attacking the notion of fraternity as a political goal on a par with liberty and equality, Malraux has argued that the experience of fraternity—much like the emotion of love—cannot be accounted for by reason: "Like the sacred, it escapes us if we extract from it its deeply irrational element. As obscure as love, like love a stranger to any sense of virtue or duty; like love—and unlike liberty—a provisional sentiment, a state of grace."[63]

The idea of fraternity that plays so central a role in Malraux's middle and late writings, like various states of mystical communion described in earlier Romantic literature, suggests a means of escaping isolation through union with a larger whole. But unlike other modes of self-transcendence, it permits the individual to preserve both his sense of discrete identity and his commitment to volitional action: Kyo's feeling of communion with his comrades, for example, enhances both his self-possession and his awareness of the meaning of his own life. Malraux's virile fraternity (like Lawrence's "star-equilibrium") thus unites two goals whose paradoxical coexistence is characteristic of Romantic thought: an affirmation of individual selfhood and a release from the bonds of the ego.

Appendix

Notes

Index

Appendix

The following assertions, excerpted from a list entitled "Some Basic Propositions of a Growth and Self-Actualization Psychology," suggest how closely Maslow's influential theory resembles D. H. Lawrence's basic doctrine:[1]

1. We each have "an essential inner nature" that is "intrinsic, given, 'natural' " (p. 190).
2. This nature provides "potentialities, not final actualizations" (p. 190).
3. It is "best to bring out and encourage, or at the very least, to recognize this inner nature, rather than to suppress or repress it" (p. 197).
4. "Each person's inner nature has some characteristics which all other selves have . . . and some which are unique to the person" (p. 191).
5. "Self-actualization is not altogether general. It takes place via femaleness *or* maleness . . . one must first be a healthy, femaleness-fulfilled woman or maleness-fulfilled man before general-human self-actualization becomes possible" (p. 210).
6. "Though, in principle, self-actualization is easy, in practice it rarely happens" (p. 204). (Cf. Lawrence: "Only at his maximum does an individual surpass all his derivative elements, and become purely himself. And most people never get there.")[2]
7. The individual's "inner core, even though it is biologically

based and 'instinctoid,' is weak in certain senses rather than strong. It is easily overcome, suppressed or repressed . . . Authentic selfhood can be defined in part as being able to hear . . . impulse-voices within oneself, i.e., to know what one really wants or doesn't want, what one is fit for and what one is *not* fit for'' (p. 191).

8. The "development toward the concept of a healthy unconscious, and of a healthy irrationality, sharpens our awareness of the limitations of purely abstract thinking, of verbal thinking and of analytic thinking. If our hope is to describe the world fully, a place is necessary for preverbal, ineffable, metaphorical, primary process, concrete-experience, intuitive and esthetic types of cognition'' (p. 208).

9. "Growth has not only rewards and pleasures but also many intrinsic pains . . . Each step forward is a step into the unfamiliar . . . It frequently means a parting and a separation, even a kind of death prior to rebirth'' (p. 204). (Cf., for example, Lawrence's poem "New Heaven and Earth" in *Look! We Have Come Through!*)

10. "We must differentiate the Freudian type of superego from intrinsic conscience and intrinsic guilt . . . Intrinsic guilt is the consequence of betrayal of one's own inner nature or self, a turning off the path to self-actualization, and is essentially justified self-disapproval. It is therefore not as culturally relative as is Freudian guilt. It is 'true' or 'deserved' or 'right and just' or 'correct' because it is a discrepancy from something profoundly real within the person rather than from accidental, arbitrary or purely relative localisms'' (pp. 194-195). (Cf. Lawrence: "Bah, the Divine Father, like so many other Crowned Heads, has abdicated his authority. Man can sin as much as he likes. There is only one penalty: the loss of his own integrity. Man should *never* do the thing he believes to be wrong. Because if he does, he loses his own singleness, wholeness, natural honor. If you want to do a thing, you've either got to believe, sincerely, that it's your true nature to do this thing—or else you've got to let it alone.'')[3]

11. ''All this implies a naturalistic system of values, a byproduct of the empirical description of the deepest tendencies of the human species and of specific individuals'' (p. 205).

Maslow indicates some familiarity with D. H. Lawrence's writings when he compares what he calls a ''peak-experience'' to a state of being described by Lawrence and other Romantic writers.[4] He seems wholly unaware, however, of the fundamental correspondence between his very conception of the self and that espoused by the Rousseauistic tradition in general and Lawrence in particular. Crediting recent developments in ''Humanistic Psychology'' with the creation of ''a new philosophy of life, a new conception of man,'' Maslow takes no account of the fact that his assumptions are rooted in two centuries of Romantic thought.[5]

Notes

Introduction

1. Lawrence's and Malraux's relationship to the Romantic movement has been studied from several perspectives very different from mine. See, for example, Herbert Lindenberger, "Lawrence and the Romantic Tradition," in Harry T. Moore, ed., *A D. H. Lawrence Miscellany* (Carbondale: Southern Illinois University Press, 1959), pp. 326-341; Colin Clarke, *River of Dissolution: D. H. Lawrence and English Romanticism* (New York: Barnes and Noble, 1969); Henri Peyre, "Malraux le romantique," *La révue des lettres modernes,* 355-359 (1973), 7-20; and Margaret Sobel, "Malraux the Romantic," *Studies in Romanticism,* 12 (1973), 551-558. Middleton Murry briefly compares Lawrence and Rousseau in "D. H. Lawrence and T. S. Eliot," *Love, Freedom, and Society* (Cape, 1957), rpt. in *J. Middleton Murry: Selected Criticism 1916-1957,* ed. Richard Rees (London: Oxford University Press, 1960), p. 290. As far as I know, the only detailed comparison of these two authors is Gregory Leland Ulmer, "D. H. Lawrence and the Rousseau Tradition" (Ph.D. diss., Brown University, 1972). Malraux's affinity with Byron has been mentioned in passing by several scholars but has not to my knowledge been systematically explored.

2. *Selected Journalism from the English Reviews by Stendhal with Translations of Other Critical Writings,* ed. Geoffrey Strickland (London: John Calder, 1959), p. 306. Stendhal attributes one other common trait to these two men: a tendency to exaggerate their own misfortunes (ibid., p. 303).

3. The title character of *Childe Harold's Pilgrimage* so closely resembles his creator that when Byron published the fourth canto of this work,

declaring himself "weary of drawing a line which every one seemed determined not to perceive," he gave up the pretext of a fictional protagonist. (See letter to John Hobhouse preceding the fourth canto of the poem.) All quotations from Byron's poems and plays are taken from *The Complete Poetical Works of Byron*, ed. Paul E. More (Boston: Houghton Mifflin, 1905).

4. In 1829 Stendhal wrote, "Lord Byron has only been able to depict one man: himself" ("Memories of Lord Byron," *Selected Journalism*, p. 297). A modern critic has reached the same conclusion. The real purpose of Byron's poetry, "from first to last," writes John Wain, "was to present the character of the poet" ("Byron: The Search for Identity," *Essays on Literature and Ideas* [London and Toronto: Macmillan, 1963], rpt. in Paul West, ed., *Byron: A Collection of Critical Essays* [Englewood Cliffs, N.J.: Prentice-Hall, 1963], p. 159).

5. For a stimulating discussion of the relationship between Rousseau's writing and his desire for public validation of his identity, see Jean Starobinski, *Jean-Jacques Rousseau: La transparence et l'obstacle* (1957; rpt. Paris: Gallimard, 1971), pp. 149-153, 216-221.

6. *Le Persifleur*, quoted in Starobinski, *Rousseau*, pp. 68-69 (my translation). In the following paragraph Rousseau suggests that "certain dominant dispositions and certain almost periodic returns" do make him to some extent predictable.

7. *Lady Blessington's Conversations of Lord Byron*, ed. Ernest J. Lovell, Jr. (Princeton, N.J.: Princeton University Press, 1969), p. 220. Conflicting indications of self-consistency and of changeability in Byron's character are discussed by Patricia M. Ball in *The Central Self: A Study in Romantic and Victorian Imagination* (London: Athlone Press, 1968), pp. 16-21.

8. *Byron: A Self-Portrait: Letters and Diaries 1798 to 1824*, ed. Peter Quennell (1950; rpt. New York: Humanities Press, 1967), I, 234.

9. The quality of "mobility" that Byron assigns to Lady Adeline in this poem may well be intended, as Patricia M. Ball suggests, as a description of his own unsteady temperament. Explaining this quality as the "vivacious versatility" of those "who are strongly acted on by what is nearest" (*Don Juan*, XVI.97), Byron adds in a supplementary note, "It may be defined as an excessive susceptibility of immediate impressions—at the same time without *losing* the past; and is, though sometimes apparently useful to the possessor, a most painful and unhappy attribute."

10. Albert J. Guerard has demonstrated that mutually contradictory im-

pulses toward self-assertion and self-dissolution not only are commonly found in the works of individual Romantic poets, but frequently coexist within a single poem ("Prometheus and the Aeolian Lyre," *Yale Review,* 33 [1943-44], 482-497). Peter L. Thorslev, Jr., goes so far as to suggest that the unresolved tension between these contradictory drives constitutes "the basis of Romantic *Weltschmerz* in all of its various guises" (*The Byronic Hero: Types and Prototypes* [Minneapolis: University of Minnesota Press, 1962], p. 89). While writers of the Romantic period give little attention to the conflicting nature of their goals, Nietzsche, perhaps their most influential heir, devotes his first major work to the coexistence of opposing impulses toward individuation and self-transcendence, to which he attributes the birth of tragedy.

11. *The Social Contract,* first published 1762, trans. G. D. H. Cole, in *The Social Contract and Discourses* (New York: E. P. Dutton, 1950), p. 15. For Rousseau, Geoffrey Hartman has observed, "nothing is more important than breaking through to individuality, unless it is breaking through individuality." Hartman proposes this fact as the reason for regarding Rousseau as the first important Romantic ("Reflections on Romanticism in France," in David Thorburn and Geoffrey Hartman, eds., *Romanticism: Vistas, Instances, Continuities* [Ithaca: Cornell University Press, 1973], p. 38).

12. *Childe Harold's Pilgrimage,* III.72-75.

13. An entry in Byron's journal suggests that the communion with nature celebrated in his poetry is sometimes far from his actual state of mind: "Neither the music of the Shepherd, the crashing of the Avalanche, nor the torrent, the mountain, the Glacier, the Forest, nor the Cloud, have for one moment lightened the weight upon my heart, nor enabled me to lose my own wretched identity in the majesty, and the power, and the Glory, around, above, and beneath me" (*Self-Portrait,* I, 356).

14. See Jacques Voisine, *J.-J. Rousseau en Angleterre à l'époque romantique: Les écrits autobiographiques et la légende* (Paris: Didier, 1956), pp. 293-304. Not at all pleased at being so often compared with Rousseau, Byron argued (on grounds rather different from mine) that he and Rousseau were in fact polar opposites: "He wrote prose, I verse: he was of the people, I of the Aristocracy: he was a philosopher, I am none: he published his first work at forty, I mine at eighteen: his first essay brought him universal applause, mine the contrary: he married his housekeeper, I could not keep house with my wife: he thought all the world in a plot against *him,* my little world seems to think *me* in a plot against it . . . he liked Botany, I like

flowers, and herbs, and trees, but know nothing of their pedigrees: he wrote Music, I limit my knowledge of it to what I catch by *Ear* . . . he had a bad memory, I *had* at least an excellent one . . . he wrote with hesitation and care, I with rapidity and rarely with pains: *he* could never ride nor swim 'nor was cunning of fence', *I* am an excellent swimmer, a decent though not at all a dashing rider . . . and was sufficient of fence—particularly of the Highland broadsword" (*Self-Portrait,* II, 607-608).

15. *Emile,* first published 1762, trans. Barbara Foxley (1911; rpt. New York: Dutton, 1969), p. 256. Assuming that all human beings are by nature good, Rousseau attributes evil to the subversion of instinct by the conscious will: "The guilty, who assert that they are driven to crime . . . fail to perceive that the weakness they bewail is of their own making; that their earliest depravity was the result of their own will; that by dint of wishing to yield to tempations, they at length yield to them whether they will or no" (ibid.).

16. Correspondence, quoted in Ronald Grimsley, *Jean-Jacques Rousseau: A Study in Self-Awareness* (Cardiff: University of Wales Press, 1969), p. 216.

17. *The Confessions of Jean-Jacques Rousseau,* written 1765-1770, published posthumously 1781-1788, trans. J. M. Cohen (Middlesex, England: Penguin Books, 1954), p. 106.

18. Ibid., p. 63.

19. Ibid., p. 270.

20. Ibid., pp. 212-213.

21. *The Reveries of a Solitary,* written 1776-78, published posthumously 1782, trans. John Gould Fletcher, Research and Source Works Series 867, Philosophy Monography Series 85 (1927; rpt. New York: Burt Franklin, 1971), p. 132.

22. Ibid., p. 43. Rousseau's stress on his own passivity can perhaps be explained in part as a strategy for self-exoneration. What concerns us here, however, is not the accuracy of Rousseau's self-portrait but the values that emerge from his personal writings.

23. *Self-Portrait,* I, 10.

24. *The Works of Lord Byron: Letters and Journals,* ed. Rowland E. Prothero (1898-1901; rpt. New York: Octagon Books, 1966), III, 405.

25. *Self-Portrait,* II, 669.

26. See Starobinski, *Rousseau,* pp. 103-104, for a discussion of this aspect of Rousseau's thought.

27. *Self-Portrait,* I, 173.

28. Ibid., I, 226. While Byron's determination generally assures the gratification of his wishes, his restlessness prevents him from enjoying any object of desire once it has been won. An entry in his journal notes, "It is odd I never set myself seriously to wishing without attaining it—and repenting" (ibid., 206).

29. While Rousseau's personal writings seem to advocate an unresisting acceptance of an intrinsic nature, his political writings suggest that modern man cannot return to a natural state but can achieve deliberate self-improvement. (For a discussion of the role of the will in Rousseau's social thought, see Ernst Cassirer, *The Question of Jean-Jacques Rousseau,* first published 1932, trans. Peter Gay [1954; rpt. Bloomington: Indiana University Press, 1963], pp. 105-108; and Marshall Berman, *The Politics of Authenticity: Radical Individualism and the Emergence of Modern Society* [New York: Atheneum, 1970], pp. 155-159.) Ronald Grimsley, *Jean-Jacques Rousseau*, suggests that Rousseau does not intend his own acquiescence to impulse to serve as a model for his contemporaries: "By an accident of birth he had been born with a temperament which absolved him from the necessity of striving for the 'virtuous' perfection which was—or should be—the object of other men's lives: his particular disposition had prevented him from being permanently corrupted by society and he had never really lost [his] pristine innocence" (p. 265).

30. Starobinski, *Rousseau*, pp. 18-22.

31. *Emile*, p. 255.

32. *The Reveries of a Solitary*, p. 163. From an Existential viewpoint Rousseau's assumption of an acquiescent stance is itself an act of deliberate self-creation. A discrepancy between Rousseau's efforts at self-definition and his implicit repudiation of volition becomes clear on the first page of *Confessions*, where his aggressive announcement of his unprecedented enterprise of self-revelation contrasts sharply with the passivity attributed to the self he is about to portray. Malraux suggests that by transforming the "pitiful shame of Jean-Jacques" into the "proud shame of Rousseau" *Confessions* exemplifies the "metamorphosis of a fate undergone into a fate transcended" (*Anti-Memoirs,* first published 1967, trans. Terence Kilmartin [New York: Bantam Books, 1968], pp. 4-5).

33. Byron's final work, the comic masterpiece *Don Juan,* represents a complete departure from the perspective of his Romantic works. The protagonist of this poem is a fundamentally passive figure who accepts without resistance whatever his destiny brings. Repudiating his former preoccupa-

tion with conscious volition, Byron goes so far as to criticize Plato for failing to acknowledge "the controulless core/ Of human hearts" (I.116).

34. *The Life of Henry Brulard*, written 1835, published posthumously 1890, trans. Jean Stewart and B. C. J. G. Knight (1958; rpt. New York: Funk and Wagnalls, 1968), pp. 146-147.

35. "Rousseau's moments of exaltation had become my customary manner of being. I took that for genius, I cultivated it complacently and looked with pity on those who didn't have it. I must keep that for myself alone, otherwise I'll be everlastingly unhappy in society" (*The Private Diaries of Stendhal,* trans. Robert Sage [Garden City, N.Y.: Doubleday, 1954], p. 174).

36. *Henry Brulard,* p. 337.

37. *To the Happy Few: Selected Letters of Stendhal*, trans. Norman Cameron (New York: Grove Press, 1952), p. 219.

38. For a fuller discussion of Julien as a Rousseauistic hero see Maurice Bardèche, *Stendhal romancier* (Paris: La Table Ronde, 1947), pp. 203-209.

39. In English literature, these conflicting perspectives coexist, for example, in the poetry and critical theory of Shelley and in Brontë's *Wuthering Heights*.

40. For a discussion of Nietzsche's influence on Lawrence see Patrick Bridgwater, *Nietzsche in Anglosaxony: A Study of Nietzsche's Impact on English and American Literature* (Leicester, England: Leicester University Press, 1972), pp. 104-109. Nietzsche's influence on Malraux has been studied from a number of perspectives. A comprehensive analysis can be found in R. Batchelor's excellent article, "The Presence of Nietzsche in André Malraux," *Journal of European Studies,* 3 (1973), 218-229. Other discussions of Malraux's debt to Nietzsche include Thomas H. Cordle, "Malraux and Nietzsche's *Birth of Tragedy,*" *Bucknell Review,* 8 (1958-59), 89-104; Blossom Douthat, "Nietzschean Motifs in *Temptation of the Occident,*" *Yale French Studies*, 18 (1957), 77-86; and Denis Boak, *André Malraux* (Oxford: Clarendon Press, 1968), pp. 211-217.

41. The phrase I quote is used by W. D. Williams, who provides an extensive analysis of Nietzsche's debt to Rousseau in *Nietzsche and the French: A Study of the Influence of Nietzsche's French Reading on his Thought and Writing* (Oxford: Basil Blackwell, 1952), esp. pp. 9-12, 20-21, 63-66, 88-89, 103-106, 126-129, 142-143, and 169-171.

42. *Ecce Homo,* first published 1908, in *Basic Writings of Nietzsche,* trans. Walter Kaufmann (1966; rpt. New York: Random House, 1968),

"Why I Am So Clever," section 4. (For ease of reference, all citations to Nietzsche's works are by section rather than page number.) Well versed in Byron's writings during his formative years, Nietzsche wrote a critical essay on the subject of Byron's dramas when he was seventeen.

43. *The Will to Power,* first published 1901-1906, trans. Walter Kaufmann and R. J. Hollingdale (New York: Random House, 1968), section 439; section 440; *The Anti-Christ,* first published 1895, trans. R. J. Hollingdale (Middlesex, England: Penguin Books, 1968), section 11.

44. *Thoughts out of Season,* first published 1874, trans. Adrian Collins (London: T. N. Foulis, 1910), part III, section 1.

45. *The Gay Science*, first published 1882, trans. Walter Kaufmann (New York: Random House, 1974), section 270.

46. *Beyond Good and Evil,* first published 1886, trans. Marianne Cowan (Chicago: Henry Regnery, 1955), section 287. The idea that one's potential self is inherent at birth lends support to Nietzsche's antipopulist views. He argues, for example, that mass education can lead only to inauthenticity: "In our very popularly-minded, i.e. rabble-minded times, education and culture *must* essentially be the art of deception—as to one's origin, one's inherited rabble in body and soul. An educator who today would preach truthfulness above all, who constantly admonished his charges to be 'true,' to be 'natural—be what you are'—even such a virtuous and well-meaning ass would learn shortly to grasp that *furca* of Horace's, in order *naturam expellere"* (ibid., section 264).

47. *Dawn of Day*, first published 1881, trans. Johanna Volz (London: T. Fisher Unwin, 1903), section 560.

48. *The Gay Science,* section 290. Each of the two conceptions of selfhood with which this study is concerned rests on the assumption that man is free to determine his mode of being—in one case by choosing whether or not to realize his true nature, in the other case by creating a freely chosen self. At times, however, Nietzsche espouses a third perspective, insisting that man in fact possesses no freedom of choice. On one occasion, for example, he argues that the very notion of free will is a fallacy that theologians perpetrate for their own ends (*Twilight of the Idols,* first published 1889, trans. R. J. Hollingdale [Middlesex, England: Penguin Books, 1968], "The Four Great Errors," section 7). Elsewhere, insisting that our actions are wholly governed by our nature, he declares, "No one is responsible for his acts" (*Human, All Too Human,* first published 1878-1879, trans. Alexander Harvey [Chicago: Charles H. Kerr and Co., 1908], sec-

tion 39). The sense of freedom that we experience when we succeed in resisting a craving is only an illusion, he argues, for our intellect is "nothing but the blind tool of another craving, a rival of that one which torments us" (*Dawn of Day*, section 109). While this deterministic view of man provides Nietzsche with a convenient weapon in his attack upon conventional morality, it becomes counterproductive when he advocates a change in man's behavior. Not surprisingly, therefore, it receives relatively little emphasis in his writings.

49. *The Genealogy of Morals*, first published 1887, trans. Francis Golffing (Garden City, N.Y.: Doubleday, 1956), section 10.

50. *The Gay Science*, section 290.

51. *The Anti-Christ*, section 57. A mean between extremes of impulsiveness and restraint is suggested by Nietzsche's praise of Goethe: "What he aspired to was *totality;* he strove against the separation of reason, sensuality, feeling, will . . . Goethe conceived of a strong, highly cultured human being, skilled in all physical accomplishments, who, keeping himself in check and having reverence for himself, dares to allow himself the whole compass and wealth of naturalness, who is strong enough for this freedom" (*Twilight of the Idols*, "Expeditions of an Untimely Man," section 49).

52. "A Dissertation on the Origin and Foundation of the Inequality of Mankind," first published 1755, in *Social Contract*, p. 270. The willingness to engage in laborious occupations is to Rousseau a symptom of civilized man's corruption. While the savage "lives within himself," social man "only knows how to live in the opinion of others" and therefore exhausts himself to win external approbation (ibid.).

53. Ibid., p. 223.

54. *Beyond Good and Evil*, section 259.

55. "Rousseau's concept of nature, as if 'nature' were freedom, goodness, innocence, fairness, justice, an idyl—still a cult of Christian morality fundamentally" (*The Will to Power*, section 340).

56. Ibid., section 1017.

57. In an essay on eighteenth-century French literature Lawrence parodies what he takes to be Rousseau's doctrine: "You must be honest in your material dealings, you must be kind to the poor, and you must have 'feelings' for your fellow-man and for nature . . . In order to get nice 'feelings' out of things, you must of course be quite 'free,' you mustn't be interfered with. And to be 'free,' you must incur the enmity of no man, you must be 'good.' And when everybody is 'good' and 'free,' then we shall all have

nice feelings about everything" ("The Good Man," *Phoenix: The Posthumous Papers of D. H. Lawrence,* ed. Edward D. McDonald (1936; rpt. New York: Viking Press, 1972), p. 751.

58. *Emile,* p. 229.

59. Ibid., p. 241.

60. Ibid., p. 243.

61. *The Will to Power,* section 124.

62. *Thus Spake Zarathustra,* first published 1883-1892, trans. Thomas Common (New York: Random House, n.d.), section 4.

Nietzsche comes quite close to anticipating Lawrence's celebration of sheer bodily life when the physicality he contemplates has nothing to do with sex. Thus, for example, his depiction of Zarathustra as a "blissfully light-spirited" dancer who "loveth leaps and side-leaps" (section 73, part 18) is paralleled by Lawrence's portrayal of the protagonist of *Women in Love* as a man who "danced rapidly and with a real gaiety" (1920; rpt. New York: Viking Press, 1960, p. 85).

63. *Thus Spake Zarathustra,* section 13. Walter Kaufmann has defined Nietzsche's ideal to be "the passionate man who is the master of his passions" (*Nietzsche: Philosopher, Psychologist, Antichrist* [1950; rpt. New York: World Publishing Company, 1956], p. 244). But insofar as sexual passion is concerned, *Thus Spake Zarathustra* reflects a very different viewpoint. In this work Nietzsche exalts those individuals who have no need to master physical desire, being "chaste . . . from their very nature." He suggests, furthermore, that chastity is commendable only in those whose sexual drive is weak: "Chastity is a virtue with some, but with many almost a vice . . . To whom chastity is difficult, it is to be dissuaded: lest it become the road to hell—to filth and lust of soul" (ibid.).

64. *The Will to Power,* section 778.

65. *Thus Spake Zarathustra,* section 18. Nietzsche's association of sexual desire and the will to power is echoed in Malraux's analysis of eroticism (see chapter 3).

66. *Beyond Good and Evil,* section 284.

67. "Study of Thomas Hardy," *Phoenix,* p. 491. The sense of "oneness with all life" that Lawrence here associates with the sexual act recalls the identification with the whole of nature that Rousseau achieved through passive reverie. Rousseau's influence on this aspect of Lawrence's thought was mediated not by Nietzsche but by English Romantic poetry. The dissolution of the individual will intrinsic to such experiences makes them anti-

thetical to the values that inform Nietzsche's writings after *The Birth of Tragedy.*

68. *Aaron's Rod* (1922; rpt. New York: Viking Press, 1961), p. 288. Lawrence subsequently suggests rather startlingly that Nietzsche's will to power is the "benevolent will, in fact, the love-will."

69. "Blessed Are the Powerful," *Phoenix II: Uncollected, Unpublished, and Other Prose Works by D. H. Lawrence,* ed. Warren Roberts and Harry T. Moore (New York: Viking Press, 1970), p. 440.

70. *Dawn of Day,* section 35.

71. "Canst thou give unto thyself thy bad and thy good, and set up thy will as a law over thee? Canst thou be judge for thyself, and avenger of thy law?" (*Thus Spake Zarathustra,* section 17).

72. *The Birth of Tragedy,* first published 1872, trans. Francis Golffing (Garden City, N.Y.: Doubleday, 1956), section 9. In *The Will to Power,* Prometheus is described as a prime example of "a species of conquering and ruling natures in search of material to mold" (section 900).

73. *Thus Spake Zarathustra,* section 69.

74. Malraux's repudiation of absurd rebellion on behalf of an active commitment to a contemporary struggle is perhaps anticipated by Byron's involvement in the Greek war for independence. Cognizant of his debt to his Romantic forebears, Malraux has responded to an interviewer's praise of his achievement of harmony between thought and action by declaring Byron to be "the prototype of the great French Romantics in that field" (*Malraux Past Present Future: Conversations with Guy Suarès,* trans. Derek Coltman [Boston: Little, Brown and Company, 1974], p. 68).

1. Stendhal

1. For a partial list of the names Stendhal gave himself, see Robert M. Adams, *Stendhal: Notes on a Novelist* (1959; rpt. New York: Funk and Wagnalls, 1968), pp. 5-6.

2. "Truth in Masquerade," trans. B. A. B. Archer, in Victor Brombert, ed., *Stendhal: A Collection of Critical Essays* (Englewood Cliffs, N.J.: Prentice-Hall, 1962), p. 117. From Jean Starobinski, *L'oeil vivant* (Paris: Librairie Gallimard, 1961). First appeared in *Les temps modernes* (October 1951).

3. The autobiographies of these two men are compared at some length

in Gita May, ''Préromantisme rousseauiste et égotisme stendhalien: Convergence et divergences,'' *L'esprit créateur,* 6 (1966), 97-107.

4. *Souvenirs d'égotisme* (written 1832, published posthumously 1892; rpt. Paris: Le Divan, 1950), p. 84. My translation.

5. *The Life of Henry Brulard,* written 1835, published posthumously 1890, trans. Jean Steward and B. C. J. G. Knight (1958; rpt. New York: Funk and Wagnalls, 1968), p. 3.

6. *The Private Diaries of Stendhal,* ed. and trans. Robert Sage (Garden City, N.Y.: Doubleday, 1954), p. 219.

7. *Lucien Leuwen,* written 1834-1835, published posthumously 1855 and 1894, trans. Louise Varèse (1950; rpt. Norfolk, Conn.: New Directions, 1961), I, 240.

8. *Henry Brulard,* p. 289.

9. *Red and Black*, first published 1830, trans. Robert M. Adams (New York: W. W. Norton and Company, 1969), p. 15. All citations from *The Red and the Black* in my text are to the Norton critical edition.

10. See Harry Levin, *The Gates of Horn: A Study of Five French Realists* (New York: Oxford University Press, 1963), pp. 102-104.

11. *Love,* first published 1822, trans. Gilbert and Suzanne Sale (London: Merlin Press, 1957), pp. 188, 220.

12. *The Charterhouse of Parma,* first published 1839, trans. C. K. Scott-Moncrieff (1925; rpt. New York: Signet, 1962), p. 80.

13. Michael Wood, *Stendhal* (Ithaca, N.Y.: Cornell University Press, 1971), p. 151.

14. See May, ''Préromantisme rousseauiste,'' p. 104.

15. *To the Happy Few: Selected Letters of Stendhal,* trans. Norman Cameron (New York: Grove Press, 1952), p. 331. (Cited hereafter as *Letters.*)

16. Correspondence quoted in Norton critical edition of *Red and Black,* pp. 430-431.

17. *Letters,* pp. 139-140.

18. A study by Geneviève Mouillaud of attitudes held by members of Stendhal's Parisian circle suggests that Stendhal's love of spontaneity owes a good deal to social as well as literary influence. Stendhal's associates all prided themselves on their originality, ingenuousness, and naturalness and spent much of their time accusing each other of affectation, a regard for conventions, and an acceptance of readymade opinions. The most common accusation was that of affected naturalness (''The Sociology of Sten-

dhal's Novels: Preliminary Research," *International Social Science Journal,* 19 [1967], 589).

19. In the second volume of *Lucien Leuwen* Stendhal makes one attempt to denigrate the elder Leuwen's urbane charm by allowing us to view his cynicism through the critical eyes of his son. But most readers will probably still find Leuwen Senior a more attractive character than his less artful but rather spineless offspring.

20. Rousseau is generally far less ambivalent than Stendhal in his preference for simplicity over artifice. But where sexual pleasures are concerned, he too concludes that civilization has greatly improved upon nature: "Seamstresses, chambermaids, and shop girls hardly tempted me; I needed young ladies . . . However it is certainly not pride of rank or position that attracts me. It is a better preserved complexion, lovelier hands, greater elegance in jewellery, an air of cleanliness and refinement about a woman's whole person, better taste in her way of dressing and expressing herself, a finer and better made gown, a neater pair of shoes, ribbons, lace, better done hair. I should always prefer the less pretty woman of two if she had more of all that. I find this prejudice most absurd myself; but my heart dictates it, in spite of me" (*The Confessions of Jean-Jacques Rousseau,* first published 1781-1788, trans. J. M. Cohen [Middlesex, England: Penguin Books, 1954], p. 132). Sexual desire might appear to be the one aspect of an individual's life most likely to be governed by instinct rather than culture. Yet it is precisely in his erotic preferences that Rousseau proves most influenced by the values of his society.

21. Elsewhere Stendhal goes so far as to suggest that when a lover is unable to exercise control over his behavior, his actions have no relation at all to his true identity: "When a being is dominated by an extreme passion, all that he says or does in a particular situation proves nothing concerning him" (*Letters,* p. 189).

22. Erich Auerbach, *Mimesis: The Representation of Reality in Western Literature,* trans. Willard R. Trask (Princeton, N.J.: Princeton University Press, 1953), pp. 481-482; George Lukács, *Studies in European Realism: A Sociological Survey of the Writings of Balzac, Stendhal, Zola, Tolstoy, Gorki and Others,* trans. Edith Bone (London: Hillway Publishing Company, 1950), p. 81.

23. See Peter Brooks, *The Novel of Worldliness* (Princeton, N.J.: Princeton University Press, 1969), p. 228.

24. A surprisingly large number of critics have denied that Julien is

actually a hypocrite at all. Wallace Fowlie, for example, writes, ''Only on the surface does Julien Sorel appear hypocritical. He is, in a profound sense, the opposite of the hypocrite. He is a crusader for a better morality, and he uses hypocrisy as the only weapon available'' (*Stendhal*, Masters of World Literature Series [London: Macmillan Company, 1969], p. 122). Taking an even more extreme position, Everett Knight argues that in Stendhal's novels hypocrisy is used only by the mediocre, never by superior men like Julien, who ''give free reign to their generosity and follow their leanings, at the risk of becoming pariahs'' (''Stendhal et André Gide,'' *French Review*, 24 [1951], 465, my translation). A more analytical case against regarding Julien as a hypocrite is made by Jean Hytier and Victor Brombert, both of whom argue that the true hypocrite is one who does not realize he is being hypocritical (Hytier, *Les romans de l'individu: Constant, Saint-Beuve, Stendhal, Mérimée, Fromentin*, Le XIXe Siècle [Paris: Les Arts et le Livre, 1928], p. 107; Brombert, *Stendhal: Fiction and the Themes of Freedom* [New York: Random House, 1968], pp. 70-71). Only a fundamentally nonhypocritical person, Brombert maintains, could decide ''from the outside,'' as Julien does, to play the role of hypocrite. This argument implies that one's true identity is determined by an intrinsic nature rather than by consciously chosen acts. Yet elsewhere in his book Brombert attributes precisely the opposite opinion to Stendhal: ''A hundred years before Malraux, Stendhal might have said that man is what he does, not what he hides. This emphasis on choice and action, this disregard for all the forces that may bind and determine, helps explain why Stendhal has been so dear to the Existentialist generation'' (p. 174).

25. On the one occasion when Julien cannot immediately justify his actual proclivities, altruism provides a convenient excuse for doing what he wants to do. Julien realizes that rationally he ought to accept Fouqué's offer of a partnership, but he is nevertheless loath to do so. It suddenly occurs to him that Fouqué expects him to become a permanent partner. ''And shall I betray my friend? Julien said angrily to himself'' (p. 59). ''This creature, for whom hypocrisy and cold calculation were the ordinary means of refuge, could not on this occasion endure the idea of even the slightest dishonorable act toward a man who was fond of him,'' the narrator explains, and then he adds, ''But suddenly Julien was happy; he had a reason for his refusal.'' Stendhal seems to be subtly suggesting here that even Julien is capable of moralistic rationalization when he does not want to examine his actual motives too closely.

26. Frank O'Connor, *The Mirror in the Roadway: A Study of the Modern Novel* (New York: Alfred A. Knopf, 1956), p. 13.

27. Governed solely by his own unyielding will, Julien is a spiritual progenitor of the title character of *Lafcadio's Adventures* by André Gide. Like Julien, Lafcadio combines rigid self-discipline with a repudiation of all conventional restraints. Both young men are so determined to hide their true nature that they inflict severe physical punishment on themselves for betraying genuine feelings. Lacking any coherent values, they both regard obedience to whim as the ultimate test of will. From the moment Lafcadio conceives of the possibility of pushing Fleurissoire from the train, this act of murder becomes his "duty" just as holding Mme de Rênal's hand became Julien's duty as soon as it occurred to him to do so. Both Julien and Lafcadio are incapable of resisting any action they perceive as a test of will and therefore, to use Gide's words, are at "the mercy of the first opportunity."

28. Perceiving the shortcomings of his society's conception of honor, Stendhal went so far as to propose a law that would punish dueling by incarceration, during which the offender was to be permitted to read only Livy, to "teach young minds that it is possible to be brave without fighting duels" (*Letters*, pp. 165-168). But, according to his cousin, Romain Colomb, Stendhal took part in several duels himself (ibid., p. 165, n. 4).

29. Starobinski, "Truth in Masquerade," p. 117.

30. *Letters*, pp. 257-258. A close parallel to Stendhal's Louaut narrative is found in Nietzsche's writing: "Let us thoroughly revolve in our minds the reason why we jump after a person who, before our eyes, falls into the water, though we do not in the least care for him . . . The mischance of another offends us; it would convict us of our impotence, perhaps of our cowardice, if we did not afford relief to it. Or it produces in itself a diminution of our honour in the eyes of others and of ourselves" (*Dawn of Day*, first published 1881, trans. Johanna Volz [London: T. Fisher Unwin, 1903], section 133). A more recent exploration of the question raised by both Stendhal and Nietzsche is found in *The Fall* by Albert Camus. Camus's narrator, Jean-Baptiste Clamence, claims that he once heard the cries of a drowning woman and made no attempt to save her. Haunted by the memory of this event, Clamence finds his former complacency shattered. Examining the motives of his earlier generosity, he finds a preoccupation with his own identity at the root of all his fine actions. But while Camus seems to parallel Nietzsche and Stendhal in his view of human motivation, he differs markedly from them in his attitude toward his per-

ceptions. Stendhal's Louaut, never having assumed himself to be altruistic, is proud to find that he cares more for his honor than for his health. Clamence, on the other hand, responds to his new self-knowledge with the bitterness of a disillusioned idealist.

31. *Le triangle noir* (Paris: Gallimard, 1970), p. 32. My translation. Not all readers have been convinced that Julien is indeed responsible for the course of his life. André Le Breton, for example, regards him as an *"impulsif,"* incapable of sufficiently mastering his heart and his nerves. He points out that Julien left Verrières only because he was ordered to do so, destroyed his future in the church by an irrational display of profane erudition, and came to the attention of M. de La Mole only by chance (Le rouge et le noir *de Stendhal*, Les chefs-d'oeuvre de la littérature expliqués [Paris: Mellottée, n.d.], p. 276). Taking a similar position, F. W. J. Hemmings writes, "Never was a young man so assured that he was shaping his own destiny, and so hugely mistaken" (*Stendhal: A Study of His Novels* [Oxford: Oxford University Press, 1964], p. 118). In the world Stendhal depicts, a penniless carpenter's son would have little hope of rising in society by his unaided efforts, but Julien surely does not owe his success to fortune alone. He is, for example, able to attend the Besançon seminary only because he has convinced Abbé Chélan of his exceptional promise, and he is introduced to M. de La Mole as a result of having earned the esteem of the demanding Abbé Pirard.

32. Eight years after writing *The Red and the Black* Stendhal planned a companion novel whose central character would be totally lacking in imagination and wholly despicable (Hemmings, *Stendhal*, p. 120).

33. Brombert suggests that Stendhal's actual attitude toward Julien can generally be deduced by reversing his apparent value judgments: terms that appear derogatory like *"sot"* or *"ridicule"* should be translated to mean "lively," "natural," "spontaneous," "generous," whereas conventional terms of approbation like *"sang-froid"* and *"prudence"* have the pejorative implications of stiffness and frigidity (Brombert, *Stendhal*, p. 69). While this is a useful rule of thumb, it of course does not resolve all ambiguities in Stendhal's portrayal of Julien.

34. For a discussion of this aspect of Stendhal's thought, see Léon Blum, *Stendhal et le Beylisme* (Paris: Albin Michel, 1947), pp. 131-133. Blum maintains that Stendhal's philosophy of life rests on a paradox, for it demands the voluntary pursuit of a happiness that is defined to be inaccessible to the will.

35. This aspect of Julien's character brings to mind Byron's empathetic analysis of Napoleon: "But quiet to quick bosoms is a hell, / And *there* hath been thy bane; there is a fire / And motion of the soul which will not dwell / In its own narrow being, but aspire / Beyond the fitting medium of desire; / And, but once kindled, quenchless evermore, / Preys upon high adventure, nor can tire / Of aught but rest; a fever at the core, / Fatal to him who bears, to all who ever bore" (*Childe Harold's Pilgrimage*, III.42).

36. Jean-Paul Sartre, "On *The Sound and the Fury:* Time in the Work of Faulkner," *Literary and Philosophical Essays,* trans. Annette Michelson (1955; rpt. New York: Collier Books, 1962), p. 92. From *Situations I* (Paris: Gallimard, 1947).

37. And boredom, as Stendhal well knew, tends to destroy all ambition, creating a vicious circle. Shortly after completing *The Red and the Black* Stendhal wrote in a letter, "I am so stunned by boredom that I no longer desire anything: my wishes extend no further than a fireplace" (*Letters,* p. 273).

38. Alfred Adler, *The Practice and Theory of Individual Psychology,* rev. ed., trans. P. Radin (New York: Harcourt, Brace and Company, 1929), p. 13; pp. 3-4.

39. I am not wholly convinced by Michael Wood's argument that we are told nothing of Julien's thoughts at this time because "he has no thoughts. His endless ratiocinations have made way for action" (*Stendhal,* p. 86).

40. A somewhat similar interpretation of Julien's crime is suggested by D. J. Mossop in "Julien Sorel, the Vulgar Assassin," *French Studies,* 23 (1969), 138-144.

41. A full account of the trial of Antoine Berthet can be found in the Norton critical edition of *Red and Black,* pp. 420-429. Maurice Bardèche provides a detailed comparison of Julien and Berthet, but concludes from the difference in their situations that Julien's crime can have no valid explanation (*Stendhal romancier* [Paris: La Table Ronde, 1947], pp. 185-186).

42. For this reason a number of critics base their view of Julien's true identity entirely on this idyllic love. D. J. Mossop, for example, regards the energetic side of Julien's nature as an "artificial personality" that culminates in his crime and then disappears, revealing a character that is naturally sensitive and gentle (pp. 143-144). Similarly, Henry Amer argues that prison teaches Julien that he was "born" for love ("Amour, prison et temps chez Stendhal," *Nouvelle revue française,* 10 [March 1962], p. 485).

171

43. Stendhal himself discovered that the very existence of the future made it impossible for him to live completely in the present. In an 1812 letter, after complaining bitterly about his current existence in Moscow, he concludes, "All this is furiously urging me to ask for the sub-prefecture at Rome. I would not hesitate, if I were sure of dying at the age of forty" (*Letters*, p. 139).

2. D. H. Lawrence

1. Victorian novelists generally regard a preoccupation with self as the sign of a reprehensible egoism. In a recent study of Victorian fiction John Halperin demonstrates that novel after novel depicts the "moral and psychological expansion" of protagonists who move from "self-absorption" to a "relatively self-denying objectivity." In the novels that Halperin discusses genuine self-knowledge is usually equated with altruistic self-abnegation (*Egoism and Self-Discovery in the Victorian Novel* [New York: Burt Franklin, 1974]).

2. *Red and Black,* first published 1830, trans. Robert M. Adams (New York: W. W. Norton and Company, 1969), p. 226; *Lucien Leuwen,* written 1831-1836, published posthumously 1855 and 1894, trans. Louise Varèse (1950; rpt. Norfolk, Conn.: New Directions, 1961), II, 343; *The Charterhouse of Parma*, first published 1839, trans. C. K. Scott-Moncrieff (1925; rpt. New York: Signet, 1962), p. 139; *Love*, first published 1822, trans. Gilbert and Suzanne Sale (London: Merlin Press, 1957), p. 84.

3. *Psychoanalysis and the Unconscious* (1921; rpt. New York: Viking Press, 1960), p. 42. Cited hereafter as *Psychoanalysis*. And *Fantasia of the Unconscious* (1922; rpt. [with *Psychoanalysis and the Unconscious*], New York: Viking Press, 1960), p. 75. Cited hereafter as *Fantasia*. The knowledge referred to here is of course not mental knowledge but what Lawrence calls "primal consciousness." The original nucleus formed at conception and containing the essence of one's identity is subsequently "embodied," Lawrence explains, in the solar plexus.

4. *Psychoanalysis*, p. 14.

5. "The Novel," *Phoenix II: Uncollected, Unpublished, and Other Prose Works by D. H. Lawrence,* ed. Warren Roberts and Harry T. Moore (New York: Viking Press, 1970), p. 423; "Democracy," *Phoenix: The Posthumous Papers of D. H. Lawrence,* ed. Edward D. McDonald (1936; rpt. New York: Viking Press, 1972), p. 711.

6. "The Reality of Peace," *Phoenix,* p. 673.

7. "Life," *Phoenix,* p. 695.

8. "The Reality of Peace," *Phoenix,* pp. 688, 670. The imagery in this passage, reminiscent of Rousseau's *Reveries,* might seem to suggest that Lawrence, too, is exalting daydream over action. But Lawrence does not share Rousseau's tendency to associate a repudiation of volition with passivity. Thus, for example, while Rousseau suggests that man in a state of nature would work only to fulfill his physical needs, Lawrence regards the desire to work as intrinsic to man's deepest self: "It is an inherent passion, this will to work, it is a craving to produce, to create, to be as God" ("Study of Thomas Hardy," *Phoenix,* p. 429).

9. *Fantasia,* p. 85. Lawrence's repeated use of "too" in this assertion has an odd ring, for by literally ascribing an excess of certain qualities to those who deviate from a fixed standard Lawrence implicitly asserts the existence of a norm at the same time that he explicitly denies it.

10. *Phoenix,* p. 512.

11. *Phoenix II,* p. 421-422.

12. *Phoenix,* p. 529.

13. "Pornography and Obscenity," *Phoenix,* p. 173.

14. *Studies in Classic American Literature* (1923; rpt. New York: Viking Press, 1964), p. 177. Lawrence's use of religious terminology to defend the notion of an identity that is independent of action is reminiscent of Nietzsche's assertion, quoted above, that an artist's or scholar's rank is determined by "faith" rather than works (*Beyond Good and Evil,* section 287).

15. *Studies in Classic American Literature,* pp. 42-43. Within Lawrence's proto-Calvinistic framework one's actions are significant largely as clues to one's essential nature, but these clues are sometimes ambiguous. Lawrence at one point suggests, for example, that the fate of a horse that threw his rider should rest on the quality in his nature that prompted his behavior rather than on the action itself: "Was it the natural wild thing in him which caused these disasters? Or was it the slave, asserting himself for vengeance? If the latter, let him be shot. It would be a great satisfaction to see him dead. But if the former—" (*St. Mawr* [1925; rpt. New York: Random House, n.d.], p. 73). Again sounding very much like Nietzsche, Lawrence suggests that a single act of violence may be admirable if it is prompted by the unfettered instinct of a free spirit, but despicable if motivated by the resentment of one born to be a slave.

16. "Why the Novel Matters," *D. H. Lawrence: Selected Literary Criticism,* ed. Anthony Beal (New York: Viking Press, 1966), p. 106. Cited hereafter as *Criticism.*

173

17. *Women in Love* (1920; rpt. New York: Viking Press, 1960), p. viii. All citations from *Women in Love* in my text are to this edition.

18. *Freudianism and the Literary Mind*, 2nd ed. (Baton Rouge: Louisiana State University Press, 1957), p. 166.

19. "The Reality of Peace," *Phoenix*, p. 677.

20. *Phoenix II*, p. 490.

21. "The State of Funk," *Phoenix II*, p. 567; *Fantasia*, p. 105.

22. "Surgery for the Novel—or a Bomb," *Phoenix*, p. 520.

23. *Studies in Classic American Literature*, p. 6.

24. *The Plumed Serpent* (1926; rpt. New York: Random House, 1955), p. 225.

25. "The Good Man," *Phoenix*, p. 752. Lawrence's repudiation of his earlier belief in man's ability to free himself from culturally determined forms of consciousness is discussed by Baruch Hochman in reference to the role of myth in Lawrence's later writings (*Another Ego: The Changing View of Self and Society in the Work of D. H. Lawrence* [Columbia: University of South Carolina Press, 1970], pp. 202-224).

26. "Democracy," *Phoenix*, p. 710. Nietzsche, too, draws a sharp distinction between an individual's true nature and his identity in the eyes of others. But he suggests that an inauthentic image of the self may in fact have its source not in an individual's deliberate self-projection, but in the misleading signals that he receives from those around him. The vast majority, he declares, base their conception of themselves not on "a real ego, accessible to and sounded by [themselves]," but on "the phantom of this ego, which has grown up in the heads of their friends and been transmitted to them" (*Dawn of Day*, first published 1881, trans. Johanna Volz [London: T. Fisher Unwin, 1903], section 105).

27. "Surgery for the Novel—or a Bomb," p. 518.

28. Letter to Edward Garnett, June 5, 1914, *Criticism*, p. 18.

29. Even Lawrence's own writings reflect the abiding power of traditional modes of thought. Baruch Hochman, *Another Ego*, has pointed out that although Lawrence tries to negate the traditional dichotomy of flesh and spirit and proclaim the "seamless unity of the radical self," he actually recapitulates the dualistic tradition in his imagery, linking the spirit with upward motion and light, the flesh with downward motion and darkness (p. 120).

30. *The Age of Suspicion*, trans. Marie Jolas (New York: George Braziller, 1963), p. 62; *Mimesis: The Representation of Reality in Western Literature*, trans. Willard R. Trask (Princeton, N.J.: Princeton University Press,

1953), p. 552. Both Sarraute and Auerbach suggest that despite superficial differences, human beings everywhere are fundamentally alike. Lawrence's opposition to this view is made clear in his essay on Whitman: "Eskimos are not minor little Walts. They are something that I am not, I know that" (*Studies in Classic American Literature*, p. 167). Lawrence, who ascribes a unique "spirit of place" to every country, as well as a unique identity to every individual, has little interest in promoting the "cultural leveling process" that Auerbach associates with modern literature.

31. "Democracy," p. 714.

32. *D. H. Lawrence: Novelist* (1955; rpt. Middlesex, England: Penguin Books, 1964), p. 157.

33. This point is noted by Stephen J. Miko, who observes that Lawrence's description of Gudrun suggests "a sensual nature under great control" (*Toward* Women in Love: *The Emergence of a Lawrentian Aesthetic* [New Haven, Conn.: Yale University Press, 1971], p. 218).

34. In "Water Party," for example, Lawrence writes, "Always this desolating, agonized feeling, that she was outside of life, an onlooker, whilst Ursula was a partaker, caused Gudrun to suffer from a sense of her own negation" (p. 157). This fear of being excluded from life plays a major role in Gudrun's relationship with Gerald: "For always, except in her moments of excitement, she felt a want within herself. She was unsure. She had felt that now, at last, in Gerald's strong and violent love, she was living fully and finally. But when she compared herself with Ursula, already her soul was jealous, unsatisfied" (p. 368).

35. Mark Schorer observes that Birkin is a more elusive character than Gerald, but ascribes this fact to Birkin's withdrawal from public life, which precludes any social objectification of his struggles (*"Women in Love,"* *Hudson Review* [Spring, 1953], rpt. in Frederick J. Hoffman and Harry T. Moore, eds., *The Achievement of D. H. Lawrence* [Norman: University of Oklahoma Press, 1953], p. 169). A more fundamental difference in Lawrence's treatment of these two characters is noted by F. H. Langman, who identifies them with contrasting literary modes: "Gerald is looked at as fixed and finite, the doomed figure of classical tragedy, Birkin as fluent and immeasurable, the existential hero of a modern novel" (*"Women in Love,"* *Essays in Criticism*, 17 [1967], 199). However, taking no account of Lawrence's conviction that the true self is an intrinsic given rather than a creation of the will, he attributes to Birkin and Ursula a Sartrean capacity for the "making of choices in a continual process of self-commitment," while blaming Gerald for "acquiescing" in his doom (p. 184).

36. As Alan Friedman demonstrates in *The Turn of the Novel,* states of fixity, finality, and completion virtually always have a negative connotation for Lawrence (New York: Oxford University Press, 1966, pp. 130-178).

37. *Phoenix,* p. 687. This essay was first published in 1917, by which time *Women in Love* had been essentially completed.

38. David J. Gordon has argued that the emphasis on psychological determinism in Lawrence's portrait of Gerald is logically inconsistent with the "moral passion" that the novel conveys. The moral burden placed on Gerald makes no sense unless he has some capacity for choice, Gordon maintains, yet Lawrence implies that Gerald is damned from birth or earliest childhood ("*Women in Love* and the Lawrencean Aesthetic," in Stephen J. Miko, ed., *Twentieth Century Interpretations of* Women in Love [Englewood Cliffs, N. J.: Prentice-Hall, 1969], p. 58). Gordon's objection is an eminently reasonable one. But the problem of reconciling determinism with moral judgment did not exist for Lawrence any more than it had for those who believed that men were saved or damned by divine predestination.

39. David Cavitch makes this point in *D. H. Lawrence and the New World* (New York: Oxford University Press, 1969), p. 68.

40. *The Rainbow* (1915; rpt. New York: Viking Press, 1961), p. 492.

41. The relationship between Gerald's fear of being tied up and the womb imagery of the novel is noted by John E. Stoll in *The Novels of D. H. Lawrence: A Search for Integration* (Columbia: University of Missouri Press, 1971), pp. 179-180.

42. *Man against Himself* (New York: Harcourt, Brace, and World, 1938), pp. 23-71.

43. *Sons and Lovers* (1913; rpt. New York: Viking Press, 1958), p. 194.

44. *The Complete Poems of D. H. Lawrence,* ed. Vivian de Sola Pinto and F. Warren Roberts (New York: Viking Press, 1971). While Lawrence repeatedly suggests an analogy between the relationship of man and woman and that of mother and infant, he sometimes claims for himself the role of progenitor. Thus a poem entitled "Birth Night" concludes, "To-night is a woman born/ Of the man in me."

45. For a perceptive discussion of Lawrence's later view of the relationship between men and women see H. M. Daleski, *The Forked Flame: A Study of D. H. Lawrence* (London: Faber and Faber, 1965), pp. 188-257.

46. The portrait of Mrs. Morel in *Sons and Lovers* may help to explain why Lawrence associates these two traits.

47. Lawrence's attempt to link Ursula's self-isolating egoism with her "Magna Mater" qualities suggests a solution to a critical controversy over the meaning of Birkin's stone throwing in "Moony." Rejecting the standard interpretation of Birkin's attack upon the moon's reflection as a protest against woman's tyrannous possessiveness, Colin Clarke regards it as an effort to shatter Ursula's egoistic isolation (*River of Dissolution: D. H. Lawrence and English Romanticism* [New York: Barnes and Noble, 1969], pp. 99-110). But since Lawrence perceives maternal possessiveness and withdrawal into the self as intimately related, Birkin's symbolic violence is presumably directed simultaneously against both.

48. In a psychoanalytic study of Lawrence, Daniel A. Weiss, attributing to Birkin a "fear of the intrauterine absorption that his friend Gerald seeks," maintains that Gerald represents Lawrence's real psychic nature whereas Birkin is merely "his dialectic personified" (*Oedipus in Nottingham: D. H. Lawrence* [Seattle: University of Washington Press, 1962], p. 103).

49. Intentionally or otherwise, Lawrence suggests a connection between Ursula's possessiveness and Birkin's desire for a masculine communion by juxtaposing his account of Ursula's determination to drink her mate "to the dregs" with the opening of "Gladiatorial," the chapter that depicts Birkin's closest approach to the union he longs for with Gerald.

50. Even earlier, in *Sons and Lovers*, Lawrence insisted that a man's relationship to his work is fundamentally different from a woman's. Paul "liked to watch his fellow-clerks at work. The man was the work and the work was the man, one thing, for the time being. It was different with the girls. The real woman never seemed to be there at the task, but as if left out, waiting" (p. 112). During his final meeting with Miriam, Paul reiterates this sexual distinction, significantly excepting himself from his generalization: " 'I suppose work *can* be nearly everything to a man,' he said, 'though it isn't to me. But a woman only works with a part of herself. The real and vital part is covered up' " (p. 416).

51. Lawrence's own contact with the "masculine" world of communal endeavor was largely limited to a rather unhappy stint as a schoolmaster, an experience that he dramatizes in a chapter of *The Rainbow* entitled "The Man's World." This world, as Lawrence depicts it, is an inhumane environment that compels the sacrifice of all individuality in the name of a mechanistic order. But although Ursula's experiences as a schoolmistress closely correspond to Lawrence's own as they are described in his poetry and

177

letters, a certain ambiguity results from the fact that he attributes these experiences to a female character. Since statements that Lawrence makes elsewhere would suggest that Ursula is acting contrary to her womanly nature in her very participation in a "man's world," her unhappiness in this world need not necessarily reflect on its capacity to fulfill the emotional needs of its rightful (male) members.

52. *Phoenix II*, p. 98. While the final text of *Women in Love* makes no explicit reference to historical circumstances, Lawrence notes in his foreword to the novel that "the bitterness of the war may be taken for granted in the characters" (p. vii).

53. Although Ursula, too, resigns her job in the community school, her resignation does not have the same symbolic significance as Birkin's, for her society would not have expected a married woman to take an active role in a public enterprise. Ursula's most significant assertion of independence from all bonds except her marriage is her repudiation of her personal past: "What had she to do with parents and antecedents? She knew herself new and unbegotten, she had no father, no mother, no anterior connections, she was herself, pure and silvery, she belonged only to the oneness with Birkin" (pp. 399-400).

54. Gordon, *"Women in Love,"* p. 57.

55. *Aaron's Rod* (1922; rpt. New York: Viking Press, 1961), p. 272.

56. The contradictions within Lawrence's political views are intelligently analyzed in Calvin Bedient, *Architects of the Self: George Eliot, D. H. Lawrence, and E. M. Forster* (Berkeley: University of California Press, 1972), pp. 161-171.

57. *Kangaroo* (1923; rpt. New York: Viking Press, 1960), p. 289.

58. In the next paragraph of the novel Lawrence attributes to Somers a dream that clearly links his pursuit of an activity that will take him "beyond" Harriet with an earlier struggle for independence from his mother's possessive love: "But Somers knew from his dreams what [Harriet] was feeling: his dreams of a woman, a woman he loved, something like Harriet, something like his mother, and yet unlike her, a woman sullen and obstinate against him, repudiating him. Bitter the woman was grieved beyond words, grieved till her face was swollen and puffy and almost mad or imbecile, because she had loved him so much, and now she must see him betray her love" (p. 94).

59. "Why should we consider ourselves, men and women, as broken fragments of one whole?" Birkin wonders. "It is not true. We are not

broken fragments of one whole. Rather we are the singling away into purity and clear being, of things that were mixed'' (p. 192).

60. Lawrence tends to attribute to the mechanical world whatever human trait he wishes to discredit at a given moment. In his essay on Whitman he identifies the tendency to merge as mechanical, discrete individuality as human (*Studies in Classic American Literature*, p. 164).

61. Through his idyllic portrayal of love in *Lady Chatterley's Lover* Lawrence appears to suggest that complete self-fulfillment can be achieved through a sexual bond in total isolation from society. Although Mellors had at one time experienced love for a man, he expresses no interest in a male communion to supplement his relationship with Connie. But an essay published in the same year as *Lady Chatterley's Lover* reiterates Lawrence's belief in a fundamental masculine need for a bond with other men: ''To satisfy his deeper social instincts and intuitions, a man must be able to get away from his family, and from women altogether, and foregather in the communion of men'' (''Matriarchy,'' *Phoenix II*, p. 552).

The Man Who Died goes even further than *Lady Chatterley's Lover* in its advocacy of individual singleness since its protagonist not only repudiates his efforts on behalf of mankind but even departs from the woman he impregnates. Lawrence suggests in this work that personal freedom can be preserved only through isolation: ''There was nothing he could touch, for all, in a mad assertion of the ego, wanted to put a compulsion on him, and violate his intrinsic solitude . . . there was no contract without a subtle attempt to inflict a compulsion'' (1928; rpt. [with *St. Mawr*] New York: Random House, n.d., p. 184).

62. *Apocalypse* (1931; rpt. New York: Viking Press, 1966), p. 198.

3. André Malraux

1. ''Morality and the Novel,'' *D. H. Lawrence: Selected Literary Criticism*, ed. Anthony Beal (New York: Viking Press, 1966), p. 108; *Anti-Memoirs*, first published 1967, trans. Terence Kilmartin (1968; rpt. New York, Bantam Books, 1970), p. 10.

2. When criticized for attributing his own patterns of thought and speech to various figures in his novels, Malraux responded, ''The autonomy of characters, a particular vocabulary given to each one . . . are not necessities . . . I do not believe that the novelist must create *characters*''

(Gaëtan Picon, *Malraux par lui-même,* Écrivains de Toujours [Paris: Éditions du Seuil, 1953], p. 38). My translation.

3. *Man's Hope,* first published 1937, trans. Stuart Gilbert and Alastair Macdonald (1938; rpt. New York: Bantam Books, 1968), p. 327; "Our Cultural Heritage," an address delivered to the International Association of Writers for the Defense of Culture, London, June 1936, trans. Kenneth Douglas, in *Yale French Studies,* 18 (1957), 37.

4. *Women in Love* (1920; rpt. New York: Viking Press, 1960), p. 184; *Aaron's Rod* (1922; rpt. New York: Viking Press, 1961), p. 111. A letter written during his final illness indicates that personal experience subsequently changed Lawrence's mind on this point: "I feel so strongly as if my illness weren't really me—I feel perfectly well and all right, *in myself.* Yet there is this beastly torturing chest superimposed on me, and it's as if there was a demon lived there, triumphing, and extraneous to me" (*The Collected Letters of D. H. Lawrence,* ed. Harry T. Moore [New York: Viking Press, 1962], II, 1211-1212).

5. *The Royal Way,* first published 1930, trans. Stuart Gilbert (1935; rpt. New York: Random House, n.d.), p. 178. All citations from *The Royal Way* in my text are to this edition.

6. This view of creativity underlies his motto, "Never trust the artist. Trust the tale" (*Studies in Classic American Literature* [1923; rpt. New York: Viking Press, 1964], p. 2).

7. *The Voices of Silence,* first published 1951, trans. Stuart Gilbert (Garden City, N.Y.: Doubleday, 1953), p. 286.

8. Ibid., p. 532.

9. Ibid.

10. Ibid., p. 543. D. H. Lawrence, one of the chief representatives of the modern tendency to "consent to the supremacy of that part of him which belongs to the dark underworld of being," is ambivalent toward primitive culture. In *The Plumed Serpent* he portrays a return to primitive roots as a source of vital energy. But in *Women in Love* he identifies "the long, long African process of purely sensual understanding" as a lapse "from pure integral being, from creation and liberty" (p. 246), and in *St. Mawr* he writes, "All savagery is half sordid. And man is only himself when he is fighting on and on, to overcome the sordidness" (1925; rpt. New York: Random House, n.d., p. 153).

11. "Postface" to *The Conquerors,* written in 1948, trans. Jacques Le Clercq (Boston: Beacon Press, 1956), p. 192.

12. *The Voices of Silence,* p. 419. Malraux does believe that in certain cases psychology can yield more honor to man the knower than it detracts from man the known. He considers the relationship between the unconscious and certain obscurities in art to be a "circumstance regarding which psychoanalysis, legitimately for once, may find much to say" (ibid., p. 590).

13. *Man's Fate,* first published 1933, trans. Haakon M. Chevalier (1934; rpt. New York: Random House, 1961), p. 241.

14. "D. H. Lawrence and Eroticism: Concerning *Lady Chatterley's Lover,*" trans. Melvin Friedman, *Yale French Studies,* 11 (1953), 56. From the *Nouvelle revue française,* January 1932.

15. Ibid., p. 57.

16. In *Women in Love* Birkin accuses Hermione of "watching [her] naked animal actions in mirrors" in order to "make it all mental" (p. 36). A similar impulse to become a voyeur vis-à-vis one's own sexual activity is dramatized in *Man's Fate* when Ferral insists on making love with the light on so that he can see his power reflected in Valérie's physiognomy. But whereas Hermione wishes to be conscious of her pleasure as she experiences it, Ferral's gratification seems to be entirely mental.

17. Gaëtan Picon, *Malraux par lui-même,* has observed that Malraux's female characters escape the role of erotic objects to be humiliated and possessed only insofar as they participate in the world of virile combat (p. 49).

18. Lawrence comes closest to Malraux's notion of eroticism in his portrayal of Gerald's desire for Minette in *Women in Love:* "Her inchoate look of a violated slave, whose fulfillment lies in her further and further violation, made his nerves quiver with acutely desirable sensation. After all, his was the only will, she was the passive substance of his will" (p. 72). But the urge for conquest that is central to Malraux's portrayal of male desire is only a superficial part of Gerald's emotional makeup, and he readily chooses Gudrun over Minette.

19. *The Temptation of the West,* first published 1926, trans. Robert Hollander (New York: Random House, 1961), pp. 52-53. All citations from *The Temptation of the West* in my text are to this edition.

20. The idea of achieving a chosen identity apparently led Malraux deliberately to suppress whatever aspects of his nature conflicted with his self-definition. Picon, *Malraux par lui-même,* observes, "He would not so often say that man must rest his identity on a chosen part of himself if he

had not had to choose, that is, to sacrifice" (p. 68, my translation). Malraux's determination to create himself in accordance with a preconceived pattern reflects his close affinity with Byron, who "put as much energy into covering up those sides of his character that wouldn't fit into the pattern, as he did into revealing the ones that would" (John Wain, "Byron: The Search for Identity," *Essays on Literature and Ideas* [London and Toronto: Macmillan, 1963], rpt. in Paul West, ed., *Byron: A Collection of Critical Essays* [Englewood Cliffs, N.J.: Prentice-Hall, 1963], p. 159).

21. See Lucien Goldmann, "Introduction à une étude structurale des romans de Malraux," *Revue de l'Institut de sociologie*, 36 (1963), 285-286.

22. In writing about a universe in which the individual creates his own values, Malraux quite wisely avoids attributing moral judgments to an omniscient narrator. But at this point his narrative technique appears unequal to his intentions, since the reader is more likely to respond with suspicion than admiration to an act of fellowship accompanied by such self-congratulation.

23. *André Malraux* (New York: Hillary House Publishers, 1960), p. 58.

24. *The Mortal No: Death and the Modern Imagination* (Princeton, N.J.: Princeton University Press, 1964), p. 317.

25. While Malraux's early heroes define the human condition largely in terms of death, Gaëtan Picon observes that life would be no more acceptable to Malraux if it were eternal, for mortality is only one of the masks assumed by "le destin"—which includes every aspect of human life not subject to man's will (*Malraux par lui-même*, pp. 73-75).

26. Malraux's views appear to have changed considerably by the time he wrote *The Walnut Trees of Altenburg*, which concludes with an assertion of the intrinsic worth of life. In this novel Malraux declares, "Oh, may victory rest with those who went to war without liking it!" a sentiment far removed from the perspective of his early novels (first published 1943 and 1948, trans. A. W. Fielding [London: John Lehmann, 1952], p. 207).

27. Malraux is haunted by Pascal's description of man's estate: "Imagine a large number of men in chains, and all condemned to death, every day some of them being butchered before the others' eyes, the remainder realizing their own plight from the plight of their fellows" (quoted in *Walnut Trees of Altenburg*, p. 222).

28. Malraux's references to suicide in *The Royal Way* suggest considerable ambivalence. Perken approves theoretically of killing oneself when one is wearing out and speaks admiringly of Grabot's determination to end

his life if things go badly. But he also declares, "Every suicide's egged on by a phantom self of his own making; when he kills himself he does it with an eye to—survival" (p. 12). Malraux here anticipates the findings of two psychologists who have concluded that the person who commits suicide is one who "cannot successfully imagine his own death and his own complete cessation" (Edwin S. Schneidman and Norman L. Farberow, eds., *Clues to Suicide* [New York: McGraw-Hill, 1957], quoted by David Bakan, "Suicide and Immortality," in Edwin S. Schneidman, ed., *On the Nature of Suicide* [San Francisco: Jossey-Bass, 1969], p. 127). By encouraging us to scorn the English doctor who suggests that Perken "finish things off" with an overdose of opium when his pain becomes too severe, Malraux seems to imply that to endure excruciating pain until death comes of its own accord is an act of will, whereas to escape from pain through suicide would be a submission. But his subsequent works portray suicide as a legitimate exercise of will: in *Man's Fate* Kyo takes poison in order to escape torture, and in *Walnut Trees of Altenburg* Vincent Berger speaks approvingly of his father's suicide, admiring "the decision with which he had *chosen* death, a death that was like his life" (p. 67).

29. *Le triangle noir* (Paris: Gallimard, 1970), p. 32. My translation.

30. *Anti-Memoirs*, p. 400.

31. In his discussion of martyrdom Karl Menninger draws a sharp distinction between legitimate self-sacrifice and pathological self-destruction, finding evidence of the latter in instances in which "the victim not only accepted his fate but gloried in it and capitalized it for his own purposes, or in which the individual deliberately sought out the means of his destruction; and those in which the element of social value, as indicated by the utility of his sacrifice, was absent or distinctly subordinate to the personal satisfactions" (*Man against Himself* [New York: Harcourt, Brace, and World, 1938], pp. 79-80). Perken's readiness to risk torture clearly meets each of these criteria.

32. Case histories of religious martyrs indicate that martyrdom frequently involves a desire to demonstrate one's fortitude either to others or to oneself—a desire closely related, according to Menninger, to overtly erotic forms of exhibitionism (ibid., pp. 119-121). Menninger illustrates this exhibitionistic impulse by citing the case of a Christian youth sentenced to a painless execution who insisted that he be tortured so that he might demonstrate "how Christians through their faith are schooled to despise death." Perken's longing for an occasion to "spit in the face of torture" would seem to have much in common with this demand.

183

33. See for example Menninger, *Man against Himself,* pp. 239, 248.

34. Menninger observes that the masochistic urge leading to what he calls "chronic suicide" tends, over time, to demand "larger and larger payments" (ibid., p. 78).

35. Perken's dying words suggest a direct contrast with Gerald Crich, who imagines himself destroyed by an external assailant at the moment of what is in fact a suicide.

36. An argument similar to mine has been proposed by René Girard. Observing that the Malraux hero takes pleasure in being "the object of some violence exerted from outside," Girard suggests that "the myth of the hero should be interpreted as the ineffective barrier which his consciousness—or rather that of the creator—tries to erect in order to hide its real motivation" ("The Role of Eroticism in Malraux's Fiction," *Yale French Studies,* 11 [1953], 52). But while I find a significant difference between *The Royal Way* and *Man's Fate,* Girard extends his generalization to all but Malraux's last two novels.

37. Everett Knight, for example, bases his analysis of Malraux's novels on the assumption that Malraux, rejecting the idea of a self entirely, believes that "nothing from either within or without is able to impose a direction upon human life" (*Literature Considered as Philosophy: The French Example* [1957; rpt. New York: Collier Books, 1962], p. 183).

38. Picon, *Malraux par lui-même,* p. 10; *Anti-Memoirs,* p. 6.

39. Sartre maintains that to be free in the philosophical sense means "by oneself to determine oneself to wish (in the broad sense of choosing)" (*Being and Nothingness,* first published 1943, trans. Hazel E. Barnes [1953; rpt. New York: Washington Square Press, 1966], p. 621).

40. *André Malraux and the Tragic Imagination* (Stanford, Calif.: Stanford University Press, 1952), p. xi.

41. In exploring the factors that make Ch'en become a terrorist Malraux is returning to a subject he pursued earlier in his portrayal of Hong in *The Conquerors.* Material conditions play a greater role in motivating Hong, who grew up hating the wealthy and respectable, than Ch'en, who did not experience poverty until the age of twenty-four. But these two characters have one thing in common: each is impelled toward violence by his exposure to a Western view of the self.

42. I have departed from Haakon Chevalier's translation here. The French text reads, "Et pas seulement aux dieux qu'il avait choisis" (*La condition humaine* [Paris: Gallimard, 1946], p. 12), which Chevalier unaccountably translates, "He was serving the gods of his choice" (p. 10).

43. I have again departed from Chevalier's translation.

44. As Everett Knight observes, Malraux's commitment to the individual will makes his works incompatible with orthodox Communist doctrine, which not only demands blind obedience from party members, but excludes personal volition from its theory of history (*Literature Considered as Philosophy*, pp. 199-200).

45. Ignoring these repeated indications of the compulsive nature of Ch'en's behavior, Everett Knight declares, "No character [is] more Gidean than Tchen of *La Condition Humaine,* who, in his every act, attempts to 'surpass' himself . . . how can we avoid thinking of Lafcadio when Tchen picks up a sliver of glass and thrusts it into his thigh?" (ibid., pp. 194-195). But Malraux makes it clear that Ch'en's stabbing of his thigh, far from being a gratuitous act of self-transcendence, is part of a pattern of compulsive behavior: " 'One always does the same thing,' [Ch'en] said to himself, disturbed, thinking of the knife he had driven into his arm" (p.198).

46. *André Malraux,* p. 18.

47. "Malraux and the Inference to Despair," *Chicago Review,* 15, No. 3 (1962), 72.

48. *André Malraux: The Conquest of Dread* (Baltimore: Johns Hopkins Press, 1960), p. 33.

49. Clappique is probably reintroduced at this point in the novel largely for comic relief. Given the brevity and insignificance of this scene in comparison with those that precede and follow it (König's interrogation of Kyo, and Kyo and Katov's death), it seems unlikely that Malraux intended the reader to place a great deal of emphasis on Clappique's final comment on personal identity. Nevertheless, the humor of this scene is not wholly without serious implications. The possibility that Malraux raises of a man with no real self at all has since been treated as a matter of central concern in Ralph Ellison's portrayal of Rinehart in *Invisible Man* and John Barth's depiction of Jacob Horner in *The End of the Road.*

50. This point is made in Avriel Goldberger, *Visions of a New Hero* (Paris: J. J. Minard, 1965), p. 208.

51. Although Ferral's sexual desires appear to be an integral part of his psychological makeup, Malraux did not originally conceive of this particular form of eroticism as the means by which a man like Ferral would fulfill his emotional needs. Rather he used Ferral as a vehicle to develop an idea that had interested him at least since 1926, when he wrote, "The entire erotic game is there: being oneself *as well as the other,* feeling one's

own sensations as well as imagining those of the partner" (*Temptation of the West*, p. 53). Later Malraux perhaps came to doubt the universal applicability of this paradigm, since he attributes this kind of eroticism to only two characters, Perken and Ferral, who share a number of other psychological characteristics.

52. This "incomparable monster, dear above all things, that every being is to himself" recalls the "awareness we have of ourselves" that Malraux described in a passage quoted above as "so veiled, so opposed to reason that any attempt of the mind to understand it only makes it disappear" (*Temptation of the West*, p. 52). At the time he wrote *Man's Fate* Malraux still perceived a universal human tendency to cherish an undefined self that has no objective reality, but he no longer believed that an individual's sense of an identity that transcends his achievements would prevent him from committing himself to any specific action.

53. In this context it is interesting to note that three years after the publication of *Man's Fate*, upon his wife's declaration of complete sexual freedom, Malraux announced the end of his own marriage. (See Robert Payne, *A Portrait of André Malraux* [Englewood Cliffs, N.J.: Prentice-Hall, 1970], p. 236).

54. Our sense of the dignity of Kyo's final moment of life is partially undercut by a subsequent description of his corpse: "He lay there, stretched out, not serene as Kyo, before killing himself, had thought he would become, but convulsed by the suffocation" (pp. 329-330).

55. *Anti-Memoirs*, pp. 4-5.

56. It is interesting to compare König with Doctor Monygham of Conrad's *Nostromo*. Both characters are filled with self-hatred by the memory of their weakness in the face of torture, but the differences between them are telling: Monygham, forced to inform on his friends, becomes obsessed with the idea of betrayal and believes that no man is trustworthy; König, made to lose all self-possession, becomes obsessed with the idea of humiliation and insists that human dignity is meaningless.

57. When Katov resolves to give away his poison, his conscious concern is not to establish his own exceptional courage but to demonstrate a generic human capacity to triumph over one's fate. This does not, however, mean that egoistical considerations play no part in his action. Malraux emphasizes the satisfaction with which Katov announces, first to the recipients of his sacrifice and then to the officer who finds them dead, that he has kept none of the poison for himself: "He had given up everything, except saying that there was only enough for two" (p. 326).

58. Each of these novels proposes an abiding union between two men as an alternative to communal participation. But while such a union remains an unattainable ideal in *Women in Love*, it becomes a reality in *The Royal Way*. It is perhaps telling that when Lawrence portrays an intimate relationship between two men, both in *Women In Love* and in *Aaron's Rod*, it is the dominant member of the pair who represents the author. Malraux, on the other hand, projects himself in *The Conquerors* and *The Royal Way* as a young, relatively inexperienced man who becomes attached to an older, more powerful figure. Widely different conceptions of their own role within a masculine union may in part explain why Lawrence had so much more difficulty than Malraux in finding the fraternity he longed for.

59. *Days of Contempt*, trans. Haakon M. Chevalier (London: Victor Gollancz, 1936), pp. 11-12.

60. Malraux's concern with human solidarity long outlasts his attraction to communism. An important scene in *The Walnut Trees of Altenburg* portrays an attempt by a German unit in the First World War to rescue the intended victims of its own poison gas attack, suggesting that in the face of the utterly inhuman a universal bond among men will transcend partisan division. In *The Voices of Silence*, however, Malraux speaks of human communion as an aspect of the past that is absent from modern life: ''The nature of this communion has varied with the ages; sometimes it instilled in man a fellow-feeling for his neighbor, for all who suffer, or even for all forms of life; sometimes it was of a vaguer order, sentimental or metaphysical. Our culture is the first to have lost all sense of it'' (p. 496).

61. For a discussion of human solitude as the central theme in Malraux's writing see Claude-Edmonde Magny, ''Malraux the Fascinator,'' trans. Beth Archer, in R. W. B. Lewis, ed., *Malraux: A Collection of Critical Essays* (Englewood Cliffs, N.J.: Prentice-Hall, 1964), pp. 117-133. From *Esprit*, 149 (October 1948).

62. *The Tragic Vision: Variations on a Theme in Literary Interpretation* (1960; rpt. Chicago: University of Chicago Press, 1966), p. 70.

63. *Lazare* (Paris: Gallimard, 1974), p. 197. My translation.

Appendix

1. Abraham H. Maslow, *Toward a Psychology of Being*, 2nd ed. (New York: D. Van Nostrand, 1968), pp. 189-214. In attempting a clear condensation of Maslow's forty-three-item, twenty-five-page list, I have changed the order in which certain points appear.

2. *Fantasia of the Unconscious* (1922; rpt. [with *Psychoanalysis and the Unconscious*] New York: Viking Press, 1960), p. 71.

3. *Studies in Classic American Literature* (1923; rpt. New York: Viking Press, 1964), p. 101.

4. *Toward a Psychology of Being,* p. 87.

5. Ibid., p. iii. Ironically, Rollo May, another leading exponent of this "new" conception of man, has singled out D. H. Lawrence to exemplify the kind of rebel who defines his ideas only negatively (*Man's Search for Himself* [New York: W. W. Norton and Company, 1953], pp. 155-156).

Index

Index

Friedman, Alan, 176n36
Frohock, W. M., 130
Gide, André, 169n27
Girard, René, 184n36
Gordon, David J., 105, 176n38
Grabot (*The Royal Way*), 122, 124-125, 127-128
Grimsley, Ronald, 160n29
Guerard, Albert J., 157-158n10
Halperin, John, 172n1
Hartman, Geoffrey, 123, 133, 158n11
Hemmings, F. W. J., 170n31
Hochman, Baruch, 174nn25,29
Hoffman, Frederick J., 73, 123
Hytier, Jean, 168n24
Joyce, James, 65, 78
Katov (*Man's Fate*), 147-148
Kaufmann, Walter, 164n63
Knight, Everett, 168n24, 184n37, 185nn44,45
Krieger, Murray, 150
Kyo (*Man's Fate*), 118, 132, 141-147, 149-150, 183n28
Langman, F. H., 175n35
Lawrence, D. H., 66-120, 145, 148-149, 153, 155; and Romantic tradition, 1, 17, 18, 19-21, 23, 25-26, 67, 78, 95, 104-105, 107, 112, 150, 164n67, 173n8. Works: "A Propos of *Lady Chatterley's Lover*," 74; *Aaron's Rod*, 20, 107-109, 110, 114, 187n58; *Apocalypse*, 111-112; "Birth Night," 176n44; "Blessed Are the Powerful," 20; "Both Sides of the Medal," 96; "Democracy," 67, 78, 81; *Fantasia of the Unconscious*, 66, 68-

69, 74, 106-107, 153; "Forsaken and Forlorn," 96; "The Good Man," 77, 163-164n57; "Humiliation," 96; *Kangaroo*, 107, 109-110, 111; *Lady Chatterley's Lover*, 71, 117, 179n61; "Life," 67; *Look! We Have Come Through!*, 96, 154; *The Man Who Died*, 179n61; "Manifesto," 96; "Matriarchy," 179n61; "Morality and the Novel," 70-71, 113; "Mutilation," 96; "New Heaven and Earth," 154; "The Novel," 67, 70; *The Plumed Serpent*, 71, 76-77, 110-111, 180n10; "Pornography and Obscenity," 72; *Psychoanalysis and the Unconscious*, 66; "Quite Forsaken," 96; *The Rainbow*, 75, 92, 104, 177-178n51; "The Reality of Peace," 67, 68, 73, 89, 92; *St. Mawr*, 173n15, 180n10; "Song of a Man Who Is Not Loved," 96; *Sons and Lovers*, 95-96, 176n46, 177n50; "The State of Funk," 74; *Studies in Classic American Literature*, 72, 76, 154-155, 175n30, 179n60, 180n6; "Study of Thomas Hardy," 20, 69-70, 103, 173n8; "Surgery for the Novel—or a Bomb," 75, 78; "Wedlock," 96; *Women in Love*, 25, 26, 71, 73, 75, 82-95, 96-103, 104-106, 109, 111, 114, 128, 142-143, 148, 164n62, 178-179n59, 180n10, 181nn16,18, 184n35, 187n58; "Why the Novel Matters," 73

190

Index